MARGARE'
REVISED AND UPDAT

Discovering
English Customs
and Traditions

SHIRE PUBLICATIONS

protection and growth of the newly sown crops. The early Christian church endorsed these ceremonies by the institution of Rogation Day, when men walked in procession to ask God's blessing on the fields and new crops, and at the same time walked the boundaries.

Many of these Rogation processions became very disorderly and were forbidden at the Reformation, but Elizabeth I granted permission for clergy, churchwardens and parishioners to walk in procession on Ascension Day to define the parish boundaries and stop at places *en route* to offer prayers for good crops. The need for impressing the boundaries upon people in this fashion was very necessary when maps were few and the populace largely illiterate. As an aid to memory, the boundary marks were beaten with willow wands, members of the party were bumped on the ground, or the boys present were themselves beaten.

In some localities these customs have survived over the years, and in others they have been recently revived, while in coastal areas, where fishing is the main industry, it is the waters that are now blessed.

Well-dressing

The decoration of their wells as a thanksgiving for the gift of

Well-dressers prepare the base board of their picture at Ashford in the Water, Derbyshire.

6

pure water was another rite performed by our pagan ancestors. Well-dressing is a survival of this ancient well worship, for the early Christians, too, knew the value of their water supplies and adapted this ritual for their own purposes. So today the decoration and blessing of wells is observed as a Christian ceremony in various places, mainly in Derbyshire. In some places it is an old and continuous tradition, but in others a recent revival or an innovation.

The decoration of the well is an intricate task in which the young as well as the old participate, so perhaps the survival of this beautiful custom is ensured. The design usually depicts a religious theme and is executed by pressing flowers and petals into clay. Weeks of preliminary preparation are necessary, but the actual making of the picture has to be delayed until the last moment. The decorated well can usually be seen for a few days after the actual blessing, if the weather permits.

Blessing the plough

The Christian church recognised four great agricultural festivals based upon the principal phases of farming: ploughing and sowing; the season of young crops and rising corn at Rogationtide; the first fruits at Lammas in August; and the final harvesting. The pagan custom of dragging ploughs through the streets and invoking the blessings of heathen gods upon them was taken over by the church, and it became customary to take a plough to church on Plough Monday (the Monday after the feast of Epiphany in January) for the blessing 'God speed the plow'.

In medieval times Plough Monday was the time when members of the Plow Guild, the trade guild whose members were concerned with tilling the soil, would go from house to house exhorting a contribution towards the Plough Light, which was kept burning in the church throughout the year. The Reformation did away with the Plough Light and church lights from other craft guilds, but in some areas the Plough Monday celebrations and collections continued.

From the latter half of the nineteenth century the Church took a new interest in the agricultural festivals of Plough Monday, Rogationtide, Lammas and Harvest Thanksgiving. The last was instigated as a church celebration by the Reverend Robert Stephen Hawker of Morwenstow, Cornwall, in 1843. In 1943 the Council for the Church and Countryside attempted to reintroduce these agricultural celebrations, and the Bishop of Salisbury drafted services for each event. For the Plough Sunday service a plough was taken into the chancel of the church, and farmers and farm workers stood by the plough while it and their work were blessed.

Clipping the Church

The origins of the ceremony known as 'Clipping the Church' are obscure. One definition of the word 'clip' is 'surround closely, grip tightly' (*Oxford English Dictionary*), and in this ceremony the church is indeed surrounded and symbolically embraced by the people joining hands and encircling the building.

Some suggest pagan origins for the custom and cite the Roman feast of Lupercalia, which apparently included a sacred dance around the altar of Lupercus and the sacrifice of young dogs. A link is made here between this and the 'puppy-dog pies' eaten at Painswick in Gloucestershire on Clipping Sunday. These pies were plum pies with little china dogs in each. However, a simpler and perhaps more plausible explanation of the custom is that it is a symbolic act of embracing the church in friendship and love.

Rushbearing and hay strewing

It has been suggested that the strewing of hay on church floors, which still occurs annually in some places, may be connected with thanksgiving ceremonies that used to follow the hay harvest. When churches had mud floors, rushes and hay were scattered for the utilitarian purpose of keeping the floor warm and dry. These would be renewed for the great feasts such as Easter, Whitsun and the church's patronal festival.

The heathen paganalia or village feasts were, once again, adapted by the early Christians and developed into the country wake – the feast of the dedication of the church. At first this was observed on the actual saint's day, and later on the nearest Sunday, and for this feast the rushes were renewed. The occasion was one of general merrymaking, with processions to the church, followed by dancing and sports. Undoubtedly there is a connection between the paganalia and the elaborate rushbearing ceremonies which still survive in northern England, and some of the intricate emblems known as rushbearings that can be seen on these occasions may be a survival from the medieval mystery or miracle plays.

Mystery plays

The original mystery or miracle plays were medieval dramas in which the story and characters were taken from sacred history or from the legends of the saints. Different scenes were allotted to the various craft guilds, whose members performed them on mobile wheeled stages. The whole production was supervised by the town authorities. Four collections of English miracle plays survive, named after the towns where they were performed: they are the York, Chester, Coventry and Wakefield (or Towneley) cycles.

A mummers' play performed in 1980 at Wilstone in Hertfordshire.

Mummers' plays

Mummers' plays are performed in various parts of England at different times of the year; according to the season, they are known by different names. Pace Egg plays are performed at Easter, the Soulcakers act their drama near All Souls' Day in November, and there are several Christmas mumming plays. They all, however, have the same central theme of death and resurrection. The principal characters are Saint (King, Prince, Sir) George, the Turkish Knight, the Doctor and Captain Slasher; various minor characters also appear, using different local names. After an introduction there is a duel and a death, and the Doctor brings the corpse to life again. These plays were transmitted orally for many generations, and odd variations have crept in, but their common origin is obvious. (Some texts appeared in chapbooks in the eighteenth century.)

Morris dancing

There is still a great deal of research going on into the origins of morris dancing. It is clear that apparent fertility or pagan connections may be either wrong or an oversimplification. There is some evidence that the morris may be connected to fifteenth-century or earlier European courtly dances. Whatever the origin, the term 'morris dance' was used locally for most ritual dances from the familiar dances of the Cotswold area to the clog processional dances of the north-west of England. The numbers and costumes of the dancers vary considerably, but there are usually six or eight men or women in a 'side', and they may be accompanied by such characters as the Hobby Horse, the Fool and Maid Marian.

Pace Egging

Eggs are traditionally associated with Easter, the egg being a symbol of continuing life and resurrection, and the custom of rolling brightly coloured eggs down a slope or hillside ('Pace Egging') is said to be symbolic of the rolling away of the stone from Christ's tomb. The word 'Pace', a form of *Pasch* or *Paques*, derives from a Hebrew word meaning 'Passover'. In many cultures eggs are symbolic of renewal of life and are associated with spring. Coloured eggs were exchanged by the Greeks, Romans, Persians and Chinese at their spring festivals, so this custom may have a pre-Christian origin.

Bonfires

Although bonfires were undoubtedly lit at the turning points of the Celtic year, a monk from Shropshire in the fourteenth century noted three types of St John's Eve (Midsummer) fires: the bonfire made of bones intended to drive away evil; the wake fire built with wood, the focal point for celebrations; and the fires composed of both bone and wood, fulfilling both functions.

The fires of 5th November are often thought to have originated from the Hallowe'en fires found in the north-west of England and in Wales. However, it is clear that the 5th November celebrations and the fires and effigy-burning are directly derived from an Act of Parliament that decreed in 1605 that the foiling of the Gunpowder Plot should be celebrated in perpetuity. There is no evidence for fire-festival celebrations at this time of year through most of England before 1605. The spread of the 5th November observance from 1606 was very slow, but by about 1625 it was found in all parts of England.

Bequests and charities

Throughout England many and various bequests were made, either of money or of the income from land, in order to help the poor, the elderly or the education of children. Such bequests were often intended to preserve the memory of the donor and to ensure

Bonfire celebrations on 5th November.

that his or her soul passed into heaven and not into purgatory. It was for much the same reason that people subscribed to the church guilds (as opposed to trade guilds): to ensure that prayers were said for their souls after their death.

Some of the bequests are distributed with due ceremony, probably instigated as a public statement of the fact of the bequest and to ensure that it is paid. Time has forced changes, as with most folk customs and traditional events, and the monetary value of the bequest has been devalued. In modern times events have been developed to raise money for charities, and some have become associated with existing observances (such as Easter or New Year), when they can take advantage of a public holiday.

Courts Leet and Baron

When law and order were maintained by the lord of the manor, before regular law courts were established, their functions were carried out by local manorial courts. Courts Baron dealt with purely manorial matters; Courts Leet dealt with criminal offences and carried out all the duties covered these days by local authorities. They appointed various officials for these purposes. Most of the places that retain these courts do so for historical and traditional reasons, but a few courts still fulfil practical functions.

11

Quit rents

A quit rent is a nominal rent that is paid by a tenant to the owner of land or property and releases the tenant from all other obligations to the owner. Thus in former times the tenant would be released from all feudal services. Many such rents have been paid for over seven hundred years, and the people concerned today often have no idea of the location of the property involved.

Revivals

In recent years there have been more and more revivals of customs and traditional practices. Sometimes the 'revival' is actually an introduction into a locality but has been so successful that the organisers continue the practice and it becomes part of the community's annual cycle of events. A revival has been included in this book if it has been enacted over a continuous period of at least ten years.

Customs of the counties

Bedfordshire

On Easter Monday greengrocers from around the **Dunstable** Downs roll oranges, which they have clubbed together to buy, down Pascombe Pit to children waiting at the bottom. This is a variation of the egg-rolling that takes place on this day in other parts of Britain. (At Preston in Lancashire oranges are sometimes substituted for eggs because they roll better.)

On the last Monday of September the **Dunstable** Statute Fair, which was originally a hiring fair, survives as a funfair.

At **Ickwell** the May Day festival has been held for four centuries. Children walk in procession to the village green for the crowning of the May Queen. There is a permanent maypole, around which some intricate and colourful dances are performed and traditional May Day songs are sung. Two 'Moggies', traditional characters in bizarre dress and with blackened faces, go round with collecting boxes.

Berkshire

The **Aldermaston** candle auction, conducted by the vicar, takes place every third year on 13th December in the village hall at 8 p.m. It is for the triennial rent of a piece of land known as Church Acre. A horseshoe nail or pin is placed 1 inch (25 mm) from the top of a tallow candle, the candle is lit, and bidding commences. When the candle burns down as far as the nail, this drops out on to an adjacent tin plate, and the highest bid made before this occurs secures the rent of the field for the next three years. The candle auction next occurs in 1998, then in 2001.

A muddy form of football unique to Eton College has been played annually at **Eton** on St Andrew's Day, 30th November, since the eighteenth century. Known as the Wall Game, it is played between teams of Collegers, scholars who live in the old college, and Oppidans, the remaining majority of full fee-paying boys, who live in boarding houses outside the college precincts. Another form of football exclusive to the College, known as the Field Game, is played at Eton in the Michaelmas Term under rules made in 1847.

Hungerford is renowned for its Hocktide celebrations on the second Tuesday after Easter. The town crier, blowing a seven-

Tutti-men and the Orange Scrambler calling at houses in Hungerford, Berkshire, during the Hocktide celebrations.

teenth-century horn, summons members to a meeting of the Manorial Court in the Town Hall. Certain officials, including two Tutti-men, are elected. The Tutti-men, carrying long staves decorated with spring flowers and topped with an orange, and accompanied by the Orange Scrambler, who has a sack of oranges, visit the houses of all the commoners, where they exact a penny toll from each man and a kiss from each woman; oranges are given in exchange. After a civic luncheon a blacksmith performs the ceremony of Shoeing the Colt – driving a nail into the shoes of visitors and new commoners. Pennies and oranges are thrown to the children, and there are various other events during the day. All this celebrates the granting of certain fishing rights to the town by John of Gaunt in the fourteenth century. The manor of Hungerford was originally owned by the Crown and was given to John of Gaunt, the founder of the House of Lancaster, in 1366. When the monarch passes through the town, he or she is presented with a red rose, the Lancastrian emblem; the present Queen received one in 1952.

The oldest surviving charity to be decided by casting lots takes place in St Mary's Church House in **Reading** on the Thursday after Easter. Three girls, all of whom have served faithfully and well in one Reading household for at least five years, draw lots for twenty nobles, left by John Blagrave in 1611.

The **Ufton Nervet** Bread Dole was established in 1581 by Lady Elizabeth Marvyn, who left money for wheat and cloth to be distributed to the poor of the parish. The dole is dispensed through the back window of Ufton Court on a date near the middle of Lent and currently consists of 161 loaves of bread and, in lieu of the cloth, several duvet covers.

At St George's Chapel, **Windsor** Castle, in June the Sovereign attends a service for the Most Noble Order of the Garter. There is a procession of the Knights of the Order in their magnificent robes.

Buckinghamshire

It is said that a fresh red flower (or red berries in winter) has been kept on the memorial to Lady Anne Lee in St Mary's church, **Aylesbury**, since her death in 1584, in accordance with the inscription on her tomb, which depicts her with three children: 'Good frend sticke not to strew with crimson flowers, This marble stone wherein her cinders rest.' However, the practice appears to be relatively recent: according to a booklet produced in 1979, her request had been honoured only 'for over a century'. *A History of Aylesbury* by Robert Gibb, published in 1855, gives a full description of Lady Lee's memorial but does not mention the red flowers.

St Martin's Day (11th November) is celebrated at **Fenny Stratford** in curious fashion every year by the firing of the Fenny Poppers. The Poppers, metal pots each weighing about 20 pounds (9 kg), are taken from the belfry of St Martin's church, where they are normally kept, to a local sports ground. They are loaded with gunpowder and fired at four-hour intervals from 8 a.m. This custom has been observed since the church was built in 1730.

An unusual custom takes place at **High Wycombe** on the third Thursday in May, when the outgoing mayor and his successor, followed by the mayoress, recorder, aldermen and town clerk, are weighed outside the town hall, beginning at around 6.30 p.m. The origins of this custom are unknown, but it is said that if a dignitary has lost weight during his or her year of office then that is a sign of diligence, but if weight is gained it is a sign of idleness.

Firing the Fenny Poppers at Fenny Stratford in Buckinghamshire.

The most famous of all pancake races takes place at **Olney** on Shrove Tuesday, and this has become an international event. It is said to date from 1445, though it has by no means a continual record. It is a race for women over sixteen who have lived in the parish of Olney for at least three months. An apron and head-covering must be worn. The course is 415 yards (379 metres) long, and the pancake must be tossed at least three times in the course of the race. The winner receives a kiss from the ringer of the Pancake Bell and a prayer book from the vicar.

Grass is strewn between the pews and along the aisles of the parish church of St Peter and St Paul at **Wingrave** on the Sunday nearest to St Peter's Day (that is, the last Sunday in June or the first in July). This is known locally as Feast Sunday, and the ceremony used to be associated with a large fair that was held on the village green but no longer takes place.

Cambridgeshire

Midsummer Fair takes place in the middle of June on Midsummer Common, **Cambridge**. The fair was granted a charter in 1211 and is traditionally opened by the mayor.

The floor of the church of St Swithin at **Old Weston**, near Huntingdon, is strewn with hay on the Sunday nearest St Swithin's Day, known locally as Feast Sunday. The hay is now bought in specially, but at one time it was cut from a local field that is said to have been left to the village for the purpose. The profits from the field are used for local charities.

When Dr Wilde died at **St Ives** he left provision in his will, dated 10th August 1675, for the income from £50 to be spent each year on Bibles, which were to be given to six children of each sex who were of 'good report, under twelve years of age and able to read the Bible'. The Bibles were to be allocated by casting dice! This ceremony is still observed on Whit Monday at noon.

When he died in 1554, John Huntingdon left money and lands to his wife on condition that 2 acres (0.8 hectare) should be planted with white peas to be distributed to the poor of **Sawston**. This charity is still in existence, overseen by the parish council; the peas are harvested in July and everyone from Sawston is entitled to a share.

At **Whittlesey**, on the weekend following Plough Monday (the first Monday after 6th January), the Whittlesey Straw Bear is paraded around the town. The Straw Bear is a man covered from head to foot in a straw costume, and he is led around the streets of Whittlesey accompanied by a musician. The custom died out in the early twentieth century but was revived in 1980 by the Whittlesey Society. The event is now a small folk festival, with morris dancers from a very wide area taking part in the procession and giving displays throughout the day.

The Whittlesey Straw Bear is paraded through this Cambridgeshire town.

Cheshire

A Soulcaking play is performed annually at the beginning of November in the village of **Antrobus**.

On the third Saturday of June at **Appleton** near Warrington the ceremony of Bawming the Thorn takes place ('bawming' means 'decorating'). Children dance around a hawthorn tree and decorate it with garlands; a procession and gala follow. The original thorn was said to be descended from the Glastonbury Thorn, which allegedly grew from Joseph of Arimathea's staff. However, in 1967 the Appleton tree fell and was replaced with a new thorn, whose ancestry is in doubt.

The **Chester** Mystery Plays were revived in 1951 and are produced as a feature of the Chester Festival of Arts. They are one of the earliest surviving cycles of mystery plays and were first performed in the early fourteenth century.

In mid May the Manley Morris Dancers, who perform the north-west clog style of morris, dance in the pedestrianised centre of **Chester**.

The Royal May Day Festival at **Knutsford**, usually held on the first Saturday in May, is the only May Day celebration in England entitled to use the prefix 'Royal', because in 1887 it was attended by the Prince and Princess of Wales. Another unique feature of this event is the decoration of the pavements with beautiful patterns and mottoes traced in coloured sand. This is a relic of a once common custom. There is a splendid procession, followed by the crowning of the May Queen and a display of maypole, morris and country dancing.

The **Lymm** May Queen Festival is celebrated on the first Saturday of June. The bounds of Lymm are beaten on Rogation Sunday (the Sunday before Ascension Day). Around the second Monday of August, in the evening, the Lymm Rushbearing Ceremony takes place, when a procession including members of the parish council, the Mayor of Warrington, morris dancers and residents of Lymm bear rushes to the parish church. On the third Saturday of December Lymm has a Dickensian Christmas Festival, when the main street is closed to traffic, stalls selling seasonal snacks and side-shows are set up, and some of the inhabitants wear Dickensian costume. Finally, at 11 a.m. on the last Saturday of every month the town crier reports the news at Lymm Cross.

The annual Rushbearing Service at **Macclesfield Forest** church (Forest Chapel), the only service of its kind in Cheshire, takes place on the second Sunday in August. Locally gathered rushes are placed on the church floor and left for a week. The service is normal evensong, but a special Rushbearing Hymn, composed at

18

the beginning of the twentieth century by a former vicar, is sung, and the sermon is preached in the churchyard.

Neston Ladies' Walking Day, usually the first Thursday in June, has been an annual event since the club was founded in 1814 as a female friendly society. Members carrying white staves topped with flowers walk in procession to the church for a service, then to the market cross for a hymn, prayer and blessing, and finally to a nearby hall for tea.

The Friday nearest 30th June is Walking Day in **Warrington**. Children from churches of all denominations take part, the town centre is closed to traffic, and shops are shut as about five thousand children, watched by about forty thousand people, walk through the town. This event was started about 1833 by the then rector, who saw the neglect and poverty suffered by children as a result of the nearby Newton races, held annually at that time. He persisted in organising this walk every year against much opposition; now the races are no longer held, but Walking Day survives.

Cornwall

The Church celebrated the feast of St John on 24th June, which coincided with the summer solstice, and the bonfires traditionally lit at this time became associated with St John's Eve. The practice of lighting midsummer fires died out during the nineteenth century but was revived in the 1920s by the Federation of Old Cornwall Societies. A chain of bonfires is lit across Cornwall soon after sunset; the fires are blessed, and wild flowers and herbs are burnt; the blessing is spoken in the Cornish language. In some places couples jump through the flames to ensure good luck.

On the first Saturday of July the **Bodmin** Riding is held; garlanded poles are carried in procession through the town by riders on horseback.

The Blessing of the Mead used to take place at **Gulval** on 24th August, the feast day of St Bartholomew, the patron saint of beekeepers and honey-makers.

Helston's May Day celebrations, better known as the Furry Dance, take place on 8th May (the feast of the Apparition of Michael) or the nearest Saturday. The streets are decorated, and various dances are performed throughout the day, commencing at 7 a.m. The principal dance, at noon, is led by the mayor, and the last dance, in which everyone joins, begins at 5 p.m.

The ancient **Marhamchurch** Revel, held on the Monday after 12th August (the feast of St Marwenne), commemorates the saint who brought Christianity to the village. The Queen of the Revel, elected from the village schoolchildren, is crowned by Father Time on the spot where the saint's cell stood. A procession round the

The Furry Dance takes place each May in Helston, Cornwall.

village ends at the Revel Ground, where there is country dancing, Cornish wrestling and amusements for all.

The 'Obby 'Oss celebrations at **Padstow** take place on May Day itself. The fun begins at midnight on 30th April, when the Morning Song is sung outside the Golden Lion inn, and a procession moves through the decorated town, singing outside each house. Later in the day the grotesque Hobby Horse appears, accompanied by the Teaser, other oddly dressed characters and a band. The Hobby

In accordance with his wishes, ten small girls dance around John Knill's monument outside St Ives, Cornwall, every fifth year.

Horse dances through the streets during the day, 'dying' at intervals until he is finally laid to rest late in the evening. Some say the Hobby Horse recalls an occasion in the fourteenth century when French raiders were frightened off by a hobby horse at the harbour entrance, and over the years this has become entangled with traditional May rites, but the explanation of the origin of this strange creature may not be quite so simple.

Hurling the Silver Ball occurs at **St Columb Major** on Shrove

Tuesday and the following Saturday week. The ball is made of wood encased in silver, and the goals are over a mile (almost 2 km) apart. The game can best be described as a violent form of rugby in which 'Town' plays 'Country', and there may be up to one thousand players in each team. If the object of the game – to score a goal – is not accomplished, then placing the ball beyond the parish boundary achieves victory.

A similar game is played at **St Ives**, traditionally on Feast Monday (the Monday of Candlemas week in February), but possibly the following Monday. The game commences at 10.30 a.m., when the mayor throws the ball from the wall of the parish church. The ball is passed from person to person as the game proceeds; whoever holds it at noon is declared the winner and receives a small prize from the mayor in return for the ball.

Every fifth year **St Ives** is also the scene of a curious ceremony that commemorates the death of a local benefactor, John Knill. It takes place on St James's Day, 25th July, and should occur next in 2001. Knill built a monument to himself on Worvas Hill, just outside the town, and left provision for ten small girls clad in white to dance round it to the tune of the Old Hundredth psalm played on a violin, the children and musician being suitably rewarded. This has become a civic ceremony, with the mayor leading a procession to the monument.

Cumbria

Ambleside Rushbearing used to take place on the Saturday nearest St Anne's Day (26th July) but more recently has been held on the first Saturday of the month, near the feast of the Visitation of St Mary, to whom the church is dedicated (2nd July). A procession of children and others carrying their 'bearings' (crosses made of rushes, wooden frames of various shapes decorated with flowers and rushes, or baskets of flowers) walks through the streets to the Market Place, where the Rushbearers' Hymn is sung. This is followed by a church service, after which gingerbread is distributed to all who take part.

The **Ambleside** Sports are held on the Thursday before the first Monday in August.

The **Appleby** Horse Fair takes place annually, beginning on the second Wednesday in June. It is a large gathering of travellers and gypsies, who come to Appleby for a week of horse racing and trading.

Until the 1920s there was a long and active tradition of mumming in the **Barrow-in-Furness** area. The players were known locally as Pace Eggers, and each village had its own particular version of the play. Many of these have been collected, and a representative text has been compiled. This is now regularly performed by some of the Furness Morris Men on Easter Saturday and Monday in a number of places in the area.

The **Egremont** Crab Fair has been held on the Saturday nearest 18th September since a charter to hold the fair was granted in 1267. The fair has nothing to do with crustaceans but is believed to be associated with crab-apples, and there are a couple of local traditions to explain the connection. Whatever the explanation, the function of the event is to mark the end of the agricultural year. Confusingly, however, there is no fair at the Crab Fair but a series of events including the Applecart Parade (when a lorry is driven slowly up the High Street and men on the back throw apples to the children), sports, including Cumbrian wrestling, the greasy pole, a pipe-smoking competition, a terrier show and the best-known event – the World Gurning Championship.

Rushbearing at **Grasmere** occurs on the Saturday nearest St Oswald's Day (5th August). A procession led by the clergy, followed by girls carrying a sheet full of rushes and by villagers, each with their rushbearing of traditional design, walks through the

The annual rushbearing procession at Warcop in Cumbria.

23

village. A special hymn is sung, and at the church, where the procession ends, rushes are arranged on the floor before a special service. Gingerbread is distributed afterwards.

The famous **Grasmere** Sports, which have taken place annually for well over one hundred years, are held on the Thursday nearest to 20th August.

The first Saturday in July is the date of the Rushbearing at **Musgrave**, where there is a procession through the village to the church, a service, tea for the children and sports.

Though the church at **Warcop** is dedicated to St Columba, the Rushbearing is held on St Peter's Day (29th June), and locally the event is known as Peter Day. The procession, headed by a band and banners, walks through the village to the church. The girls carry or wear crowns of flowers built on wooden or wire frames; boys carry crosses made of rushes. In the church these are placed on the floor round the altar, where they remain over the following Sunday; then they are hung at the back of the church until a few days before the next Peter Day. After the service there is tea followed by sports.

There is a lively game of street football played in **Workington** on Good Friday, Easter Tuesday and the Saturday following. The two teams are known as Uppies and Downies.

Derbyshire

Of all the traditions and customs still observed in this county well-dressing is undoubtedly the most famous, and rightly so, for the 'dressed' wells are a most beautiful sight. The first well-dressing of the year occurs around the second week of May at **Etwall**, a practice begun here in 1970. Nine wells are dressed at **Wirksworth** over the Spring Bank Holiday, and the five wells at **Tissington** are dressed at Ascentiontide. June well-dressings include **Ashford in the Water**, **Youlgreave**, **Tideswell** and, at the end of the month, **Hope**. In July the event takes place at **Buxton** and Marsh Lane near **Eckington**. In August there are well-dressings at **Bonsall**, **Stoney Middleton**, **Bradwell**, **Barlow**, **Eyam** and, right at the end of the month, **Wormhill**, where the event carries over into the beginning of September. Exact dates may be obtained from the Peak Park Information Centre, Bakewell.

The lead-mining industry in the Peak District is controlled by the Barmote Courts. These courts, which are the oldest industrial courts still extant in England, have powers to deal with all disputes concerning lead mining and ownership of mines; they record the ore obtained, for payment of dues and tithes. The Barmote Court at **Wirksworth** meets in April and October, and the court at **Eyam** usually meets the previous day.

A well decorated with flower petals at Stoney Middleton, Derbyshire.

A religious event that has been held for at least three hundred years takes place on the first Sunday in July near Ladybower Reservoir. This is the **Alport** Castle Woodlands Love Feast. At a time when nonconformists were heavily penalised, they met in this lonely place to hold services, and Methodists have met here ever since. There is a service in the morning, and in the afternoon at the Love Feast worshippers testify what their religion means to them and receive a small piece of cake and a sip of water from the loving cup.

The famous **Ashbourne** Shrove Tuesday football is still played. Two teams compete, the Up'ards (those born to the north of the Henmore stream, which divides the town) and the Down'ards (those born to the south of the stream). The goals are set 3 miles (5 km) apart, and play may go on until after midnight, if a goal is not scored earlier.

The ceremony of Clipping the Church is observed at **Burbage** church near Buxton during the morning service on the Sunday nearest to the date of the church's dedication in 1851, 2nd August. This is usually the last Sunday of July.

At **Castleton** on 29th May (Oak Apple Day), in the evening, the escape of Charles II from the Roundheads is commemorated with a procession. The 'King' and the 'Queen', both on horseback, lead the way. Part of the King's costume consists of a huge garland made of flowers and foliage that almost envelops him. When the procession reaches the churchyard the garland is removed and placed on top of the church tower, where it remains for about a week. It appears that at some time older May Day rites became associated with the celebrations of Charles's escape.

On the last Sunday in August a Plague Commemoration Service is held in the Dell at **Eyam**. This recalls the action of the villagers who, when the plague struck the village in 1665-6, isolated them-

The garlanded 'King' rides around Castleton in Derbyshire.

26

selves from the outside world, at the instigation of the rector, and thus prevented the spread of the disease to the surrounding district.

The Shrove Tuesday pancake races at **Winster**, which have been run since at least 1870, are open to all and take place at 2 p.m. There are small prizes for the winners.

Towards the end of June, on Wakes Saturday, the **Winster** Morris Men perform. They are the only team to perform the Derbyshire morris, a cross between the well-known Cotswold morris dances and the north-western morris tradition.

On the Sunday following 8th September the parishioners of **Wirksworth** perform their Church Clipping.

Devon

At **Ashburton** officials appointed at the meetings of the local Courts Leet and Baron in November tour the town sometime in July for the annual ale-tasting ceremonies. The Portreeve, ale-tasters and others visit the inns to taste the ale, and if it is satisfactory the landlord receives a sprig of evergreen to put over his door. Bread-weighing ceremonies are also held.

Andrew's Dole is still distributed annually on 1st January to the poor and aged in **Bideford**; John Andrew, who died in 1605, left a plot of land so that the rent from it could be used for this purpose. This money is augmented from the mayor's Christmas Appeal Fund, and a loaf of bread and half a pound (227 grams) of butter are given to anyone over sixty.

Bideford's Manor Court, which commenced in the 1880s when the manor was conveyed to the aldermen and burgesses of the borough, meets once a year on the Saturday after Easter to hear suggestions from local people for improving the town and to appoint the People's Churchwarden. The Beat the Clock Race, in which competitors tried to race across the bridge while the clock struck eight, no longer takes place since the clock stopped and the bridge was closed for repairs. Instead, there are junior and senior Around the Town races on the eve of the regatta.

The **Chawleigh** Friendly Society holds its annual club walk and feast on the first Saturday in June.

The **Exeter** Plough Sunday Service, on the first Sunday after 6th January, is held in the cathedral in conjunction with the Young Farmers. A plough is drawn from the great west door to the space before the Golden Gates, where it is blessed.

The old custom of 'Tiptoeing' is still observed at **Gittisham**. On Shrove Tuesday children go to all the houses in the area chanting 'Tip tip toe, please for a penny, then we will go'. They divide the money received between them.

'Tiptoeing' in Gittisham, Devon, on Shrove Tuesday.

The annual conker contest held on the Wednesday nearest 20th October at the New Inn, **Goodleigh**, near Barnstaple, is played with locally collected conkers, and often over one hundred contestants participate.

On the Wednesday nearest 5th November a fire carnival is held at **Hatherleigh**. The event begins around 5 a.m. with about twenty men pulling a sledge containing three blazing tar barrels through the town to a bonfire at New Market car park. During the day there is a meeting of the hunt, a horse fair, children's fancy dress, a funfair and a carnival parade led by a large torch in the shape of a cross, accompanied by flaming torches. At around 8.30 p.m. a second sledge of flaming barrels is taken through the town. The day is rounded off with a carnival discotheque.

Holsworthy Pretty Maids Charity was instigated by the Reverend Thomas Mayrick, who in 1841 left a sum of money to be invested in government stock; the interest, then about £2 10s 0d (£2.50) was to be paid annually to a single woman under the age of thirty who is 'generally esteemed by the young as the most deserving, the most handsome, and the most noted for her quietness and attendance at church'. The recipient now receives £5 and is presented to the town on the second Wednesday of July, which is the

Burning tar barrels are carried around Ottery St Mary on 5th November.

first day of the Holsworthy St Peter's Fair. Her first duty is to pay an official visit to the fair. The Holsworthy Court Leet meets on the eve of the fair.

Honiton Fair in mid July is opened by the town crier proclaiming that 'The glove is up' and that 'No man shall be arrested until the glove is taken down'. This refers to the gilded leather glove attached to the end of his garlanded pole. (The proclamation of the **Exeter** Lammas Fair on the Tuesday before the third Wednesday in July is also accompanied by the raising of a glove.)

On Good Friday at **Ideford** the Borrington Dole is distributed. The rector and churchwardens stand at one end of the tomb of Bartholomew Borrington and lay twenty shillings on its flat top. The beneficiaries come one by one to the opposite end and pick up their money.

At **Ipplepen** beating the bounds takes place at irregular and infrequent intervals. The last two beatings were in 1910 and 1950. A member of the party making the ten-hour hike is bumped on the boundary stones. One of the attractions at the village show held on the third Saturday in July is maypole dancing, and the ancient distribution of the Feo Fee money still takes place annually at Christmas.

The annual Ram Roasting Fair takes place at **Kingsteignton** on the Spring Bank Holiday Monday. It is said that this originated from a time of drought when a ram was sacrificed in the dried-up bed of the Fairwater Spring and torrential rain resulted. A ram is roasted at the Spring Bank Holiday Fair, and the meat is distributed to holders of winning programme numbers. Another feature of the fair is maypole dancing.

Maypole dancing occurs at **Lustleigh** on the first Saturday in May. It takes place in a large orchard, called Town Orchard, which in 1966 was bequeathed to the village for ever.

At **Ottery St Mary** on 5th November young men amuse themselves by carrying burning tar barrels about the town.

The giant **Paignton** Pudding is made to celebrate special events, and portions are available for all comers. The institution of the new Borough of Torbay in 1968 was such an occasion.

The curiously named Fyshinge Feast, held annually at **Plymouth** on a convenient date in June or July, commemorates the bringing of water to the town in 1590 from the river Meavy by Sir Francis Drake and the annual 'Survey of the Works and the Head Weir', which used to be essential to ensure that the tinners were not diverting the town's water supply for their own uses. The council and guests meet on the lawn by the head weir; they toast the memory of Drake in river water, and they toast his descendants in mulled ale, that they may 'never want wine'. Luncheon, including grilled trout from the Burrator Reservoir, is served at the head of the lake.

The Turning of the Devil's Boulder, when a large rock lying under an ancient oak tree in the square at **Shebbear** is turned over with great ceremony every 5th November, is said to be one of the oldest annual customs in England; if this stone, allegedly dropped by the Devil, is not turned once a year ill luck will befall the village.

A Court Leet and Court Baron are held on the third Wednesday of November at **Sidbury** Manor, near Sidmouth.

The **Tavistock** Goosey Fair, formerly a week-long fair for the buying and selling of geese, is held during the second week of October.

Widecombe Fair, immortalised in song, is held on the second Tuesday of September at **Widecombe in the Moor**.

Dorset

13th May is Garland Day at **Abbotsbury**. Two garlands, one made from wild flowers and the other from garden flowers, are paraded around the village by children, and the householders give contributions to the garlanders. At the end of the morning the garland of cultivated flowers is placed on the war memorial whilst the one made from wild flowers is abandoned. The garlands are bell-shaped structures, each about 2 feet (60 cm) high, and are carried between two children holding a pole pushed through the middle. In the days when Abbotsbury had a fishing fleet Garland Day coincided with the opening of the mackerel season. The adults of each boat-owning family would make a garland, and the children would show these round the village. They were then taken to a service in the church and then to the beach, where the fisher families would have a party and games. In the evening the garlands were attached to the bows of the fishing boats and taken out to sea. At one time, apparently, the garlands would be thrown into the sea, but this has not happened within living memory.

For over three hundred years the Court of Purbeck Marblers has met on Shrove Tuesday at **Corfe Castle** for the election of officers and the initiation of apprentices. Each of these boys has to convey a quart of beer from the Fox inn to the town hall, where the court is held, while the Marblers try to upset it. If it reaches its goal intact, the apprentice becomes a freeman of the court on payment of a fee. After the meeting, in order to preserve an ancient right of way to Ower Quay, from which the marble used to be shipped, a football is kicked along the old road.

In 1925 a local man left some money in his will to ensure the

May garlands on display at Abbotsbury in Dorset.

31

continuation of the custom of Shroving by the schoolboys at **Durweston**. Provision was also made for flowers to be laid upon his grave. In 1993 the local headmistress changed the custom slightly so that the flowers are given out to passers-by as the children sing a Shroving song.

At **Mudeford**, near Christchurch, the annual Blessing of the Waters takes place from a boat offshore.

The Perambulation of the Bounds of the Island and Royal Manor of **Portland** takes place every seventh year and is next due in 2002. The Court Leet of the Royal Manor does this on Ascension Day; at their annual meeting in November they are concerned mainly with the commoners' rights and the common land of the island.

The distribution of Christmas Pennies at **Sherborne** Castle, which apparently originated in the eighteenth century, is still made on Christmas morning. On the night before the Michaelmas Fair, held on the Monday after 10th October, 'Teddy Rowe's Band', comprising cow's horns, dustbin lids, pans and anything else that can make a noise, performs around Sherborne.

On the evening of 1st January the **Symondsbury** mummers perform their play around the local public houses.

On the third Sunday in July there is a procession to commemorate the **Tolpuddle** Martyrs, organised by the TUC South West Region. Six agricultural labourers from Tolpuddle organised themselves into the first trade union in 1834; this was regarded as a conspiracy in restraint of trade, and they were transported to Australia. After widespread agitation they were later granted a free pardon.

The Court Leet at **Wareham** carries out its inspections of the local traders' weights and measures on the four evenings before the last Friday in November.

Durham

In **Durham** curfew is rung every evening at nine o'clock, except on Saturdays, for there is a legend that a man once went alone to ring the bell on a Saturday evening and disappeared, never to be seen again. The singing of anthems from the cathedral tower on 29th May is in honour of the restoration of Charles II; originally it took place on 17th October to commemorate the victory of the battle of Neville's Cross in 1346, when Queen Philippa, in the absence of her husband Edward III in France, repelled a Scottish invasion. The monks' contribution to the battle was the singing of mass from the tower for an English victory and the promise of a special annual mass if the Queen was victorious.

Despite the reduction in size of the coal industry, the **Durham**

Miners' Gala, which was started in 1871, still takes place on the third Saturday in July, albeit on a much smaller scale than previously. Members of miners' lodges march into the city carrying banners and accompanied by bands; they congregate on the riverside racecourse, where amusements are provided for all tastes. A Miners' Festival Service is held in the cathedral.

At **Seaham Harbour**, **South Shields** and **Sunderland** it is customary for Sunday-school children to walk round the town on Good Friday. The Seaham parade has been held every year since at least 1899 and the Sunderland parade since 1850.

On Shrove Tuesday **Sedgefield** is the scene of a Shrovetide football match. The goals, a stream and a pond, are situated 500 yards (457 metres) apart. The game commences at one o'clock when the verger throws a specially made ball into the air. A general melée ensues, and the game finishes as soon as a goal has been scored.

At Easter in some parts of the county eggs which have been hard-boiled and dyed are rolled on the grass or 'jauped'. The eggs are held in the player's hand and hit against each other until they break.

Essex

The opening of **Colchester**'s oyster fishery takes place on a variable date in September. The mayor, town clerk and mace-bearer, in their ceremonial dress, travel to Brightlingsea with members of the council. From here they go by boat to Pyefleet Creek, where oysters are fattened, and an Ancient Proclamation is read declaring the fishery open for the season. All present partake of gin and gingerbread, the loyal toast is drunk, and the mayor makes the first dredge of the season. Towards the end of October (about 20th) the Oyster Feast takes place. This was already an old custom at the time of Charles II, connected with the opening of St Denys's Fair.

The ceremony of the **Dunmow** Flitch Trials is held in mid June every leap year, to reward couples who manage to live in matrimonial happiness for at least a year and a day. The origins of the custom are obscure: it is said that it dates back to 1104, when Lady Juga Baynard founded Little Dunmow Priory, but other historians suggest that it was originated by Robert Fitzwalter in the thirteenth century. The event has a chequered history, but since 1949 several trials have been held. A mock court, presided over by a judge and with a jury of six spinsters and six bachelors from Dunmow parish, conducts the trial of claimants.

Maldon Mud Race takes place on New Year's Day. This is a charity event in which participants race across the mud of the river Blackwater. In 1997 the race was postponed until later in the year because New Year's Day was so cold.

Sailing-barge races have been held at **Southend** for over one hundred years. They now take place in August from the end of the pier. There are only thirty-six of these vessels still in full commission. The annual Whitebait Festival in September originated in the early eighteenth century and was revived in 1934. A service for the Blessing of the Catch, attended by the mayor, takes place in the morning off the pier, and the fish caught are served at a dinner in the evening.

Thaxted is well-known for its connections with morris dancing. The village side, formed in 1911, was one of the first revival morris sides and since 1934 has hosted an annual meeting of morris dancers from all over England on the first weekend of June. Apart from touring the locality at Easter and Whitsun, the dancers' other main appearance is at the church's patronal festival in mid June. The dancers, sometimes with other invited morris sides, carrying boughs and other greenery, process through the village, leaving the school around 7.30 p.m., dancing at all the pubs and outside the Guildhall. About 10.15 p.m. they reach the church, where they perform the Abbots Bromley Horn Dance (see under Staffordshire).

Gloucestershire and Bristol

When Queen Matilda fell in love with the lord of the manor at **Avening** and was rejected she had him put in prison, where he died. Regretting her action, she caused the church to be built, attended its consecration in 1080 and afterwards gave a great feast, at which wild boar was served. Nowadays, after evensong in the church on the Sunday following Holy Cross Day (14th September), 'pig-face sandwiches' are served in a suitably transformed village hall, recalling the feast. On Pig-face Day, as it is known locally, these sandwiches may also be obtained at the local inns.

At **Bisley** the well is dressed on Ascension Day with garlands in the form of stars of David, letters and numbers. A short service is held, concluding with the blessing of the well by the vicar. Restored in 1863, the Bisley well is an impressive structure with five gabled water chutes, each of which is decorated for the occasion.

On August Bank Holiday Monday **Bourton-on-the-Water** is the scene of a five-a-side game of water football played in the river Windrush. This game was first played to celebrate the coronation of Edward VII.

On the Tuesday after Easter the choirboys of St Michael's

church, **Bristol**, partake of large buns known as Tuppenny Starvers. This distribution, which has been made for over two hundred years, probably started as a treat for the choir in the days when poorer people ate only black bread.

Under a bequest dated 1493 the floor of St Mary Redcliffe church, **Bristol**, is strewn with rushes on Whit Sunday, and a memorial sermon is preached at a special service attended by the Lord Mayor, who goes in procession to the church, accompanied by other civic officials. This event commemorates a wealthy merchant of the city who restored the church in the fifteenth century and later became a priest.

The annual Redcliffe Pipe Walk occurs in October. Permission granted in the twelfth century for the ministers of St Mary Redcliffe, **Bristol**, to convey water to the church via a conduit from a well, known as Rugewell, is commemorated when the vicar and parishioners walk the course of the pipe.

The ruin of St Anne's Well was acquired by **Bristol** Corporation in 1924, and on or about 25th July annually the clergy and parishioners of St Anne's church, Brislington, make a pilgrimage to this shrine, thus reviving an old custom.

An Indian pilgrimage is made annually on 27th September to the tomb of Rajah Ram-Mohun Roy in Arnos Grove Cemetery, **Bristol**. He came to Britain in 1831 as the representative of the King of Delhi and died in 1833.

Cooper's Hill near **Brockworth** is the venue for a cheese-rolling contest on Spring Bank Holiday Monday. This is a survival of a 500-year-old ceremony that preserves the grazing rights of the villagers of Brockworth-on-the-Hill. A large cheese is rolled down the hill, chased by the contestants; the winner keeps the cheese and receives a small money prize.

On the Friday after the Spring Bank Holiday 'Robert Dover's Olimpick Games', a revival dating from 1951, are held at **Chipping Campden**. This is followed the next day by the Scuttlebrook Wake, when the new May Queen is enthroned by the previous year's queen; then there is dancing round the maypole, and the Chipping Campden Morris Men perform.

The Verderers' Court of Attachment of the Forest of Dean meets every three months in the Speech House Hotel at **Coleford**. Many of its duties have been curtailed, and it now deals mainly with matters arising out of encroachment on Crown lands.

The **Cranham** Feast and Ox Roast, which lasts for three days, finishing on the second Monday in August, originated when the people asserted their common rights by publicly roasting a poached deer.

The mummers' play performed annually on Boxing Day at

Marshfield was revived in 1929. The players wear a distinctive costume which covers them from head to foot with paper streamers.

Clipping the Church at **Painswick** takes place on the Sunday nearest 19th September. The children, choir and clergy of the parish church and its daughter churches walk in procession round the churchyard; finally they join hands, encircling the church completely, while a special Clipping Hymn is sung. Buns are then distributed to the children, in place of the traditional 'Dog Pie'.

St Briavels has the distinction of being the scene of what is popularly believed to be the oldest unbroken custom in the county. On Whit Sunday after evening service the vicar and church-wardens throw small cubes of bread and cheese from a platform on the church wall to people assembled for the ceremony. Before 1860 the ceremony took place inside the church. However, the authorities considered the scramble that occurred to be unseemly and moved the event first into the churchyard and later to the road outside the church. This 700-year-old event retains for the village the right to gather firewood in Hudnalls Wood.

The costumes of the mummers at Marshfield in Gloucestershire are made from paper streamers.

Stow-on-the-Wold Fair, which was granted a charter in 1476, is held around mid May. It started as a sheep fair but over the years has developed into a horse fair that attracts gypsies and travellers from all over England.

Hampshire

A once common custom was the hanging of a 'maiden's garland' (usually a paper crown decorated with rosettes) in church on the death of a young bachelor or spinster of good character. Old garlands may still be seen in some churches, but at **Abbotts Ann** the custom is still maintained.

The villagers of **Cheriton** and nearby **Tichborne** receive flour every Lady Day (25th March) under an 800-year-old bequest. The famous Tichborne Dole originated when on her death bed Lady Mabella Tichborne requested her husband to bequeath some land for an annual distribution of bread to the poor. He consented to give as much land as she could walk round carrying a burning faggot before this became extinguished. She managed to crawl round an area of over 20 acres (8 hectares). The land, still known as the Crawls, was set aside for this purpose, and the distribution has been made ever since.

The mumming play at **Crookham**, which has been performed for at least a century and probably much longer, may be seen annually on Boxing Day. Many of the players are dressed in paper strips, but Father Christmas wears traditional red and the Doctor a top-hat and frock-coat.

Lyndhurst Verderers' Court meets every two months in open court and privately in the intervening months (except in August, when no meeting is held) in the Verderers' Hall in the Queen's House at Lyndhurst. The court regulates the exercise of common rights, supervises the welfare of depastured stock and controls development to ensure that the traditional character of the New Forest is maintained.

The Trafalgar Day ceremonies at **Portsmouth** on 21st October include a service on board HMS *Victory* when a wreath is laid on the spot where Nelson fell.

Southampton preserves several old traditions. The first day of May is greeted by carols, sung from the top of the Bargate by the choir of King Edward VI School. This event was revived around 1960. On the first Tuesday of October the sheriff and other dignitaries parade around the boundaries of the city beating the bounds. This is followed by a meeting of the Court Leet at the civic centre.

The Hospital of St Cross in Winchester still distributes the Wayfarers' Dole to visitors.

In August a bowls tournament, inaugurated in 1776 and played annually ever since, takes place for the Knighthood of **Southampton** Old Green. It usually lasts three days and is supervised by the Knights of the Green, who appear in ceremonial dress, wearing their medals of rank inscribed 'Win it and wear it'. The original rules are still observed.

Stockbridge also retains its Courts Leet and Baron, which meet annually in the spring. The courts control grazing on the Marsh. Amongst the officers appointed is a hayward, whose duties include looking after the common ground.

On 7th October 1753 William Davies became lost in the fog while returning home to **Twyford**. When he heard the bells of the church he changed his direction and thus avoided falling down a chalk pit. In his will he made provision for a feast for the Twyford bellringers in perpetuity, provided that the bells are rung morning and evening on this date. This custom has been observed without a break, except during the two world wars. The feast is now paid for by the Shipley estates.

The famous Wayfarers' Dole is still distributed daily to all who ask at the gatehouse of the Hospital of St Cross in **Winchester**. For over eight hundred years travellers have received a small square of bread and a drink of ale, until the day's supply has been used.

Herefordshire

Members of the **Fownhope** Heart of Oak Friendly Society meet annually on Oak Apple Day (29th May) or the following Saturday and parade to the church carrying their club sticks, which are decorated with wooden oak-apples and flowers.

To encourage the residents of **Hentland**, **Sellack** and **King's Capel**, near Ross-on-Wye, to live together in peace and goodwill, Lady Scudamore made provision in her sixteenth-century will for them to partake of cakes and ale communally on Palm Sunday. Ale is no longer provided, but the lady's wishes are still observed by the distribution of Pax Cakes to the congregation. Each cake bears an impression of the Paschal Lamb and is handed to the parishioners at the end of the service on Palm Sunday with the traditional greeting 'God and good neighbourhood'.

Apple wassailing on Old Twelfth Night (17th January) has been reintroduced at **Much Marcle** by local cidermakers. Cider is poured on to the tree roots, and the trees are cheered and implored to provide a good crop in the coming year. Guns are then fired through the branches.

Hertfordshire

Barnet Fair is held on the first weekend of September. It is now mainly a funfair, but originally it was the main livestock fair for the area, and some horse-trading is still carried on.

On the nearest Sunday to 20th June, St Alban's Day, there is a Rose Service at the cathedral at **St Albans**. During the service children parade with roses to the shrine of St Alban, the flowers are blessed and tossed on to the floor.

Isle of Man

The Tynwald Ceremony occurs on or about 5th July. There is a service in St John's church, **Peel**, after which the Lieutenant-Governor leads a procession of officials up a hill said to be made of earth from all the island's seventeen parishes. From the top of the hill the island's laws are proclaimed in Manx and English. This ceremony must be observed before any of the laws made by the Tynwald, the island's parliament, become effective.

Between 5th and 15th July, the day depending on the state of the tides, the **Peel** Viking Festival is held. This is a re-enactment of the conquest of the island by the Vikings: 'Vikings' land from longships; there is a battle between them and the 'Celts' in which

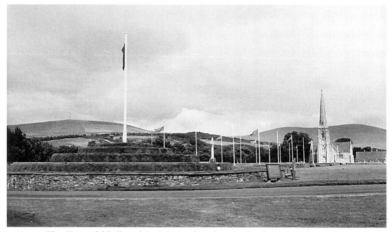

The Tynwald hill and St John's church near Peel on the Isle of Man.

the 'Vikings' triumph; a 'king' is elected, and there is a torchlight procession and firework display.

Kent

Eliza and Mary Chulkhurst were Siamese twins who lived at **Biddenden**. When they died they bequeathed 20 acres (8 hectares) of land, the income from which was to be used for a distribution of bread and cheese to the poor. This dole is still distributed on Easter Monday morning. In addition, Biddenden cakes, a kind of hard biscuit stamped with a representation of the two sisters and the date 1100, are available to all who ask for them. The date of birth of the twins is in dispute: though the cakes are stamped 1100, the year 1500 is thought by some to be a more probable date.

The tolling of the great bell, known as 'Bell Harry', occurs daily at **Canterbury** cathedral at 9 p.m. The thirteenth-century Burghmote Horn, formerly used to summon the citizens to assemblies and meetings, is sounded by a soldier of the regiment stationed at the barracks before the newly elected Lord Mayor makes his acceptance speech. The horn may also be sounded on other civic occasions, such as the appointment of a Freeman of the City. Every weekday at 11 a.m. a soldier turns a leaf of one of the books bearing the names of the fallen of the Royal East Kent Regiment. These are kept in the Warriors' Chapel (St Michael's) in the cathedral.

The Biddenden twins are portrayed on the village sign in Kent.

The annual Blessing of the Fisheries service at **Folkestone** takes place in mid afternoon on the first Sunday in July. At **Margate** a similar service is held in January by the local Greek community to celebrate Epiphany. The Greek Orthodox Archbishop of Thyateria and Great Britain takes part. During the service a crucifix decorated with flowers is thrown into the water, to be retrieved by a hardy bather.

On the second Saturday of May **Hayes** Common, near Bromley, is the venue for the largest May Queen festival in Britain. May Queens and their attendants from all over England are present at the event, and London's May Queen is crowned.

Hythe Venetian Fete has been held every second year since 1854 on a half-mile (800 metre) stretch of the Royal Military Canal, commemorating the fact that the Napoleonic invasion expected in 1804-5 never occurred. There is a ceremonial progress of the mayors of the Cinque Ports Federation on a pontoon accompanied by decorated floats. The next fete is in 1999.

On or near 16th September there is a procession to St Edith's Well at **Kemsing**; the water from the well is said to be good for

41

curing eye complaints.

The ceremony of the Blessing of the Cherry Orchards, which occurs at **Newington,** near Sittingbourne, every May, is of comparatively recent origin. After a service of dedication in the church the congregation proceeds to a nearby orchard, where the actual blessing takes place.

The popular medieval sport of tilting the quintain now survives only at **Offham**. The quintain, permanently positioned on the village green, consists of a post with a sandbag attached. The sandbag swings round to strike an unskilful tilter. This spectacle may be witnessed at the May Day celebrations, in addition to maypole dancing. The tilters are mounted on horseback, and a bucket of water replaces the sandbag.

The mayor of the city of **Rochester** was appointed Admiral of the Medway in 1446 by royal charter, and in this capacity he carries out certain duties. Once a year, on the first Saturday in July, the Admiralty Court, which was established by Act of Parliament in 1728 and is concerned with the administration of the oyster fisheries, meets in a decorated barge moored off the pier, attended by the mayor. He or she walks in procession with civic and other

Participants in the summer Dickens festival at Rochester.

dignitaries, fully robed, from the Guildhall to the barge and returns after the court has closed.

Each June **Rochester** holds a Dickens festival, when the streets are filled with people in nineteenth-century costume.

Each year on 24th August there is a service in St Bartholomew's chapel, **Sandwich**, followed by a distribution of buns and biscuits, for which the children have to run around the outside of the chapel.

The **Whitstable** Blessing of the Sea takes place on Reeves Beach during the Oyster Festival week at the end of July. The blessing is on the Thursday nearest 25th July, the feast day of St James of Compostella, the patron saint of oysters. The Oyster Festival, although featuring modern events such as quizzes, indoor bowls and a discotheque, is rooted in celebrations for St James's Day. By the eighteenth century these had become the Whitstable Regatta, featuring races for working boats.

Lancashire

On Easter Saturday **Bacup** is the venue for the Nutters' Dance, performed by the Britannia Coconut Dancers. Eight men attired in black, except for white stockings, kilts and caps, and with small wooden discs (the nuts) attached to their waists, hands and knees, dance their way through the town, clapping the nuts to a musical accompaniment. The origin of this event is obscure.

Clitheroe is the second oldest chartered town in Lancashire, having been granted its charter in 1147. In May the annual Cockles and Mussels Feast is attended by the mayor and members of the council. This is followed by the mayor-making ceremony, when the outgoing mayor and deputy mayor, two halberdiers in red robes and the Town Sergeant, also in red robes and carrying the mace, process around the town from the town hall, led by the town crier and two mounted police officers. The procession is repeated with the new mayor.

The perambulation of the bounds of **Lancaster** is first recorded as taking place in 1682. Until relatively recently it was carried out every seven years in May or June, originally with the mayor and bailiffs accompanied by a trumpeter, flag-bearer and a posse of townsfolk. In the twentieth century the boundaries were perambulated by a pioneer, who was met by the mayoral party at key points on the route. During the perambulation the horseshoe set in the roadway at Horseshoe Corner, said to have originally been a shoe cast by John of Gaunt's horse, was renewed. In 1974 the larger district given to the City of Lancaster was considered too big for the traditional riding, so instead the John o' Gaunt Morris

Men danced at certain points on the boundary. The most recent perambulation took place in 1993, the eight hundredth anniversary of the borough, and the ceremony is likely to be repeated only on special occasions. Since pedestrianisation the horseshoe wears out much more slowly and is replaced when necessary.

The Travice Dole is distributed on Maundy Thursday at **Leigh**. Forty poor people come to the tomb of Henry Travice to receive five shillings each.

Manchester's Whit Walks are probably the best-known of all the religious walks that became a feature of life in the north of England in the nineteenth century. In 1969 the Roman Catholic Walk occurred on Whit Sunday and the Church of England Walk on Spring Bank Holiday Monday. Both are gala occasions, with bands and banners forming part of the huge processions.

Preston is famous for its egg-rolling in Avenham Park on Easter Monday. Every twentieth year since 1562 the Preston Guild Merchant has been held for a week in early September. The balls, banquets and civic parades are only incidental to the historic ceremonies of the Guild Court, which are still maintained. Because of the Second World War it did not take place in 1942, but it was revived in 1952.

On Whit Friday **Saddleworth**, near Oldham, is the centre for Whit Walks and an ecumenical service attended by people from the surrounding villages. The processions take place in the morning; the afternoon is given over to games and sports, and then from about 5 p.m. the brass and silver bands take part in contests in the surrounding villages. The Saddleworth Rushbearing, organised by the local morris men, was revived in 1975 and takes place on the second weekend after 12th August.

Leicestershire

The Statute Fair at **Ashby de la Zouch** was originally a hiring fair, where labourers went to find employment. It is now a funfair, which causes the main street to be blocked for four days ending on the Tuesday nearest 20th September.

On the Sunday nearest 29th June, known locally as Hay Sunday, the floor of **Braunstone** church is strewn with hay. Local legend relates that a former lord of the manor made a legacy of hay to the parish clerk as a reward for finding his daughter. This entitled the clerk to take the hay from Holm Meadow, Aylestone, and lay it in the church. Today this meadow is the site of a local gasworks, but British Gas East Midlands makes an annual payment in lieu of the hay.

At **Hallaton** Bottle Kicking and Hare Pie Scramble on Easter Monday slices of hare pie, blessed by the vicar, are thrown to the crowd at Hare Pie Bank. Then three small casks, two of which are filled with beer, are kicked or manhandled by teams from Hallaton and nearby Medbourne in an attempt to get them across their own boundary.

A 'plough play', an East Midlands form of mummers' play, was reintroduced at **Hinckley** in 1986 and is performed a week after Twelfth Night. Traditionally it was performed on Plough Monday, the Monday after 6th January.

On Midsummer's Day the landlord of the Crown and Thistle public house in **Leicester** ceremonially pays a rent of 4d (old money) and a damask rose to the Lord Mayor. The money, however, is handed straight back to the landlord.

In 1786 William Hubbard left one guinea a year forever to the church choir of St Mary in Arden, **Market Harborough**, on condition that they sang the Easter Hymn over his grave on Easter Eve. This hymn-singing still takes place in the churchyard of the now derelict church.

The custom of selling the grass verges for grazing cattle, sheep and horses has taken place at the Gate Inn, **Ratcliffe Culey**, on the Thursday in Easter week for many years; this is known as 'Spring Setting the Lanes'.

An annual distribution of oranges is made by the vicar under the old elm tree in **Sileby** churchyard on the Sunday-school anniversary, towards the end of May. The origin of this custom is obscure, but it is thought to be a revival of an ancient distribution.

Lincolnshire

On Mayor's Sunday in June there is a civic service in St Botolph's church, **Boston**, attended by the mayor, the honorary freemen of the borough, councillors and the mayor's chaplain, amongst others. The procession to the church is led by the superintendent of police, and the mayor is accompanied by the macebearer, carrying the council's official mace, and four special constables carrying the two oar maces and two halberds. At the lunchtime reception that follows in the assembly rooms the health of the mayor and the mayoress/consort is proposed by the guest of honour, who is chosen by the mayor.

On 10th December each year the Beast Mart is proclaimed under a charter granted to **Boston** corporation in 1573 by Elizabeth I. The proclamation takes place at noon in the playground of the local grammar school, where the Mart was formerly held. It is read by the town clerk in the presence of the mayor, and the pupils are granted a half-holiday, symbolic of the times when the school had to be closed during the Mart.

A curious race has been run at **Bourne** every Easter since 1770. In that year Richard Clay left a piece of land to be let each year, so that the rent would be used to purchase bread for the poor. A number of boys race over a fixed distance; as soon as they set off, an auctioneer invites bids from people who wish to rent the field. These have to be made while the boys are running, and the last bid before the boys return to the starting point is the successful one.

On the first Monday after 4th October a sheep fair, which has been in existence for over 750 years, is held at **Corby Glen**, near Grantham.

A strange will made by an inn landlord at **Grantham** provided the sum of forty shillings *per annum* for ever for an annual sermon to be preached 'wherein the subject shall be chiefly against drunkenness'. The sermon is still delivered under the terms of the bequest on the evening of Mayor's Sunday.

The ancient **Haxey** Hood Game is played annually on 6th January. It originated in the thirteenth century when the hood of Lady de Mowbray blew away as she was riding home from church and was retrieved by twelve labourers. This so amused the lady that she gave a piece of land, still known as the Hoodlands, to the village; the rent was to pay for a leather hood to be contested for annually for ever by twelve men dressed in scarlet. The game, as it is played today, resembles a debased form of rugby football; it is organised and supervised by twelve men known as 'Boggans', a 'King' and a 'Fool', all of whom wear colourful costumes. After the opening ceremonies a canvas 'hood' is thrown to the crowd; the person who secures this, eludes the Boggans and takes it to the nearest inn, receives one shilling. After twelve canvas hoods are thus disposed of, the thirteenth, made of leather, is thrown. A general melée ensues and eventually this hood, too, reaches one of the local inns. Then the game is over, free drinks are dispensed, and the hood remains here until the next year.

Until 1938 the grazing rights of a field known as Poor Folks' Close in **Old Bolingbroke** were let annually by pin and candle auction, and the proceeds were distributed to the poor on St Thomas's Day. This land is now administered in a different manner, but the tradition of the candle auction continues, for when the King George V Playing Field was left to the parish council it was specified that the grazing on this land should be let annually by the ancient method. A pin is placed in a candle not more than 1 inch (25 mm) from the top, the candle is lit, and bidding for the grazing commences; whoever makes the last bid before the pin falls is accepted as the purchaser. This auction takes place at the annual parish assembly in March.

London

Royal events

The Sovereign or her representative, accompanied by the Yeomen of the Guard, attends the Royal Epiphany Service at the **Chapel Royal**, St James's, on 6th January. Three purses, symbolising the gifts of the Three Wise Men, are presented, and afterwards their contents are distributed to the poor of the parish.

On the Thursday before Good Friday the Royal Maundy Money, specially minted for the occasion, is distributed by the Sovereign. This used always to take place in Westminster Abbey, but nowadays it happens at a different church or cathedral each year somewhere else in the country.

At Trooping the Colour on the second Saturday in June (the Queen's official birthday) the colours of one of the five Foot Guards regiments are trooped before the Queen on **Horse Guards Parade**. Afterwards the Queen proceeds to Buckingham Palace at the head of her Guards.

The Royal Horse Artillery fires a royal salute in Hyde Park.

The first Royal Tournament was held in 1880. This annual event takes place at **Earl's Court** in July, and branches of all three services present displays.

After a general election and before each new session of Parliament in mid November the Queen attends the State Opening of Parliament, a ceremony dating from the mid sixteenth century. She travels in procession from Buckingham Palace to the **Palace of Westminster**, where she reads the Speech from the Throne in the House of Lords. A few hours before this the cellars of the Houses of Parliament are searched by the Beefeaters to ensure that no latter-day Guy Fawkes lurks there.

Royal salutes of forty-one guns are fired in **Hyde Park** by the King's Troop of the Royal Horse Artillery and at the **Tower of London** by the Honourable Artillery Company, who fire an additional twenty-one guns for the City of London. These salutes are fired on various occasions throughout the year: the anniversary of the Queen's Accession, 6th February; the Queen's Birthday, 21st April; the anniversary of the Coronation, 2nd June; the Duke of Edinburgh's birthday, 10th June; the Queen's official birthday, the second Saturday in June; and the Queen Mother's birthday, 4th August.

On state occasions, when the Sovereign has to enter the City of London she is met at the site of the **Temple Bar**, the City boundary, by the Lord Mayor, who surrenders the Keys of the City to her before she proceeds. The Temple Bar was removed in 1878.

Daily events

The Changing of the Guard at **Buckingham Palace** occurs at 11.30 a.m. The Guard, accompanied by a band, marches from Wellington or Chelsea Barracks, and the band plays in the forecourt while the Guard is changed. Mounting the Guard in **Whitehall** takes place at 11 a.m. on weekdays and 10 a.m. on Sundays.

The Bank Guard or 'Picquet', instituted in 1780, is mounted daily at the **Bank of England** at 4.30 p.m., but as the soldiers arrive by coach there is little ceremony to see.

The Ceremony of the Keys takes place in the **Tower of London** at about 9.50 p.m. The Chief Warder locks up the Tower for the night and conveys the keys to the Resident Governor; Last Post is sounded. Tickets to view this ceremony are limited to seventy per night, and as there is a heavy demand it is necessary to apply to the Constable's Office as far in advance as possible.

Irregular events

The distribution of the Farthing Bundles at the Fern Street Settlement, Tower Hamlets, is no longer a regular event. It formerly took place on the first Saturday of each month, but today it happens only on special occasions. The Farthing Bundles are distributed to children small enough to pass under an archway inscribed 'Enter now ye children small, None can come who are too tall'. The children receive a bundle of small toys or trinkets in return for a penny.

Annual events

6th January. The cast at Drury Lane Theatre consume cake and wine as directed in the will of the comedian Baddeley, who died in 1795.

8th January or the first Sunday after. The Chaplain of Clowns preaches a sermon and recites a prayer over the grave of Joseph Grimaldi, the clown, by the former St James's church, Pentonville; a wreath is laid.

30th January. Wreaths are laid on the statue of Charles I at Charing Cross to mark the anniversary of his execution.

End of January. There are celebrations to mark the Chinese New Year.

3rd February. St Blaise, whose festival this is, is the patron saint of throats. At the church of St Etheldreda, Holborn, the ceremony of Blessing the Throats has taken place for over one hundred years.

First Sunday in February. Holy Trinity church, Dalston, is the venue of the annual Clowns' Service, held since 1946 to commemorate the great clown Joseph Grimaldi.

7th February. To mark the birthday of Charles Dickens, the mayor of Southwark places a wreath on the bust of the novelist outside the Charles Dickens School, Southwark.

20th February. The annual memorial service for Sir John Cass is held on or near this day at St Botolph's church, Aldgate. He died of a haemorrhage while making his will in 1718, and scholars of Sir John Cass College attending the service wear red quills in his memory.

Shrove Tuesday. At Westminster School 'Pancake Greaze', a pancake is tossed over a bar, and boys scramble for a piece; the one who obtains the largest receives a reward.

Ash Wednesday. Under a bequest in the 1612 will of John Norton, members of the Stationers' Company process from Stationers' Hall to St Faith's Chapel in the crypt of St Paul's Cathedral to hear a special sermon. On returning to their hall they partake of cakes and ale.

14th March. At the Trial of the Pyx, coins from the Mint are sent to Goldsmiths' Hall, where they are tested for weight and fineness by a jury of members of the Goldsmiths' Company.

Mothers' Day. At a revival of a ceremony dating from Tudor

49

Above: Muffled drums in the procession to Charing Cross to mark the anniversary of the execution of Charles I on 30th January.

Left: The Chinese New Year at the end of January is celebrated in London's Leicester Square.

The Clowns' Service at Dalston on the first Sunday in February commemorates Joseph Grimaldi.

Druids celebrating the spring equinox on Tower Hill.

times, young persons receive flowers and Simnel cakes at a service in the Chapel Royal at the Tower of London.

21st March. Druids meet on Tower Hill to celebrate the spring equinox.

28th March. To commemorate the restoration of the bells of St Clement Danes in 1919, a service is held in the church at 3 p.m., followed by a distribution of oranges and lemons to the children present.

Good Friday. After morning service in the church of St Bartholomew the Great, Smithfield, twenty-one widows of the parish collect a bun and sixpence from the top of a tomb in the churchyard.

Good Friday. The Widow's Son inn, Bow, recalls a Good Friday many years ago when the son of a widow was expected home from sea, so she put a hot cross bun aside for him. He never came, but she continued to keep a bun for him each year. Every year a bun is now added to the collection hanging from a bag in the bar, and there is a general distribution of buns to patrons of the inn.

Easter Sunday. Parade, Battersea Park.

Easter Monday. Harness Horse Parade in Regent's Park.

5th April. A memorial service to John Stow, the historian (1525-1605), attended by the Lord Mayor and Aldermen, is held in the church of St Andrew Undershaft on or near the anniversary of Stow's death. During the service a new quill is placed in the hand of Stow's statue.

Second Wednesday after Easter. At a special service in the church of St Lawrence Jewry the annual Spital Sermon is delivered by a diocesan bishop nominated by the Archbishop of Canterbury. The Lord Mayor and Aldermen attend. This sermon dates from before the Fire of London and has its origins in the sermons preached on the subject of the Resurrection on the Monday, Tuesday and Wednesday after Easter from an open-air pulpit cross in the churchyard.

Last Sunday in April. Commemorating the martyrs of religious persecution in the sixteenth and seventeenth centuries, a Roman Catholic pilgrimage follows the route taken by victims from Newgate Prison (Old Bailey) to the gallows at Tyburn (Marble Arch).

Ascension Day. When the bounds of St Clement Danes parish are beaten, one of the boundaries in the river Thames has to be reached by boat, and a choirboy is lowered by his heels to reach a mark in Temple Gardens.

Ascension Day. Approximately every fifth year the Bounds of the Manor and Liberty of the Savoy are beaten, following a service in the Queen's Chapel of the Savoy at 10.45 a.m. During the procession one of the choristers stands on his head several times.

Ascension Day. Every third year (the next occurrence is in 1999) the bounds of the Tower of London are beaten. After a service at 6 p.m. in the Chapel Royal of St Peter ad Vincula, a colourful procession makes its way round the thirty-one boundary marks. The choirboys strike each one with willow wands.

21st May. Henry VI was murdered in the Tower on this date in 1471. In a private ceremony each year, after a short service, the Provosts of Eton College and King's College, Cambridge, lay Eton lilies and white roses on the plaque said to mark the spot where the murder occurred in the Wakefield Tower. This tradition was begun by Eton College in the 1920s and King's College joined in the ceremony in 1947; Henry VI was the founder of both institutions.

Last Wednesday in May. At the annual Pepys Commemoration Service at noon in the church of St Olave, Hart Street, a laurel wreath is laid in front of the diarist's memorial in the church.

29th May. This is Oak Apple Day and was Founder's Day at the Royal Hospital, Chelsea, though for convenience the ceremony is now held on a Friday morning in early June. The Chelsea Pensioners parade for inspection in their colourful uniforms, and all wear a sprig of oak. They give three cheers for their founder, Charles II, whose statue is decorated with oak boughs.

Corpus Christi Day (around the end of May). The new Master and Wardens of the Skinners' Company take officers of the company and pupils from Christ's Hospital School, the Girls' School and the Judd and Skinners' School in procession from Skinners' Hall to the church of St James Garlickhythe, Skinners Lane. Posies are carried by the Tutor, the Clerk, the Master, the preacher and the four Wardens.

Beating the bounds of the Tower of London on Ascension Day.

Cutting the Knollys Rose at All Hallows by the Tower on Midsummer Day.

Midsummer Day. An annual fine of a red rose, to be presented personally to the Lord Mayor, was imposed on Sir Robert Knollys in 1346 when he built a small bridge over Seething Lane, to connect two of his properties, without planning permission (even in those days). In 1924 this payment was revived, and the church-wardens of All Hallows by the Tower present a red rose to the Lord Mayor every year.

24th June. The election of two Sheriffs and other City officers takes place on this day (unless the date falls at a weekend) with much pageantry at Guildhall. The Lord Mayor and other officers attend a church service at St Lawrence Jewry before proceeding to the Guildhall, where members of the livery companies are assembled.

Second Wednesday in July. About noon members of the Vintners' Company process from their hall in Upper Thames Street to the church of St James Garlickhythe for a service. A wine porter, dressed in top-hat and smock, sweeps the path clear with a birch broom. He is followed by the newly installed Master, the Wardens, Chaplain and Clerk, carrying nosegays, and members of the court and livery.

Third week in July. Members of the Grocers' Company attend an

The election of Sheriffs of the City of London takes place annually on or near 24th June.

annual service in the company's church following the election of the Master and Wardens for the ensuing year.

Third week in July. Swan Upping and the marking of the swans on the river Thames is performed by the Queen's Swanmaster and the Swanmasters of the Dyers' and Vintners' companies over a period of about a week. All the swans on the river from London Bridge to Henley-on-Thames are owned either by one of these livery companies or by the Queen, and the birds are counted and marked according to their ownership.

Late July. The race for Doggett's Coat and Badge occurs on a variable date, depending on the state of the tides on the Thames. This event was instituted in 1716 by an Irish actor, Thomas Doggett, who made provision in his will for it to be an annual event. There are six finalists, and the race is rowed over a 4.5 mile (7.24 km) course from London Bridge to Cadogan Pier, Chelsea. The winner receives an orange coat with a large silver badge on the sleeve.

August Bank Holiday. Notting Hill Carnival.

Around 21st September. Boys from Christ's Hospital school, Horsham, march from London Bridge station to St Sepulchre's church, High Holborn, for a service at about 11 a.m. Afterwards they go to the Mansion House, where they are received by the Lord Mayor. They are accompanied by the school band.

A wine porter sweeps the pavement in front of the members of the Vintners' Company on the second Wednesday in July.

Around 23rd September. A Druid ceremony is held on Parliament Hill Fields at midday to celebrate the autumn equinox.

28th September. The Sheriffs elected in June take office at a ceremony in Guildhall. The Lord Mayor, aldermen and others go from the Mansion House to attend this event.

29th September. The election of the new Lord Mayor takes place at noon. The present Lord Mayor goes to the Guildhall for the election of his successor, walking in procession from Guildhall to the church of St Lawrence Jewry and returning across Guildhall Yard.

The Quit Rents Ceremony at the Law Courts in October.

First Sunday in October. At 11 a.m. the Harvest of the Sea Thanksgiving Service is held in the church of St Mary-at-Hill, Lovat Lane. At 3 p.m. the Costermongers' Harvest Festival, held at St Martin-in-the-Fields, is attended by the Pearly Kings and Queens in full costume.

16th October or near. The Lion Sermon is preached at the church of St Katherine Cree, Leadenhall Street, traditionally at 1.15 p.m., to commemorate the deliverance of a London merchant, Sir John Gayer, from a lion when he was travelling in Arabia. He was buried in the church in 1694 and left money for this annual sermon.

21st October. The battle of Trafalgar is commemorated, and wreaths are laid at the foot of Nelson's Column in Trafalgar Square.

21st October or near. The Quit Rents Ceremony takes place at the Law Courts. The City Solicitor pays the Queen's Remembrancer a billhook, a hatchet and two faggots of wood for some land in Shropshire called The Moors, though the location of this land is no longer known. A second payment consists of six horseshoes and sixty-one nails, paid annually since 1234 for the site of an old forge near St Clement Danes church.

Members of the Honourable Artillery Company take part in the Lord Mayor's Show.

Last Wednesday in October. Officials of the Worshipful Company of Basketmakers attend a special service at the church of St Margaret Pattens, Eastcheap, at noon.

Second Saturday in November. The Lord Mayor's Show: the new Lord Mayor, elected in September, takes office. He travels by coach from Guildhall to the Law Courts, where he takes the oath before the Lord Chief Justice at noon, returning by coach after the ceremony. His coach forms part of a procession of floats and lorries, all decorated with a common theme, which varies from year to year. This popular event is over 750 years old and attracts great crowds.

Second Wednesday in December. A Boar's Head Feast, similar to that at Oxford, is held by the Worshipful Company of Cutlers at Warwick Lane.

Early December. The annual Cheese Ceremony is held at the Royal Hospital, Chelsea, attended by the Governor and staff of the Royal Hospital, Chelsea Pensioners and members of the National Dairy Council and related bodies. The National Dairy Council presents cheeses to the Royal Hospital, which provides beer for the Pensioners present.

Christmas Day. Members of the Serpentine Swimming Club, formed in 1864, race for the Peter Pan Cup.

Norfolk

Bede House, **Castle Rising**, is a hospital for widows and spinsters founded by the Howard family in 1614. The residents wear a distinctive costume of red cloaks and Jacobean hats, which may still be seen when they attend church on Sundays.

At **Cawston** there is an annual Plough Sunday service, usually held a few weeks after 6th January.

King's Lynn Mart is traditionally opened by the mayor in his chain of office, accompanied by the sword-bearer and mace-bearers in uniform. Mayors of other East Anglian towns also attend.

In medieval times many pilgrimages were made to the shrine of Our Lady at **Walsingham**. The Anglican shrine at the new church built in 1931 and the Roman Catholic shrine just outside the village are still visited by pilgrims throughout the summer. Of particular note are the pilgrimages to the Anglican shrine at Whitsun, and to the Roman Catholic shrine on the first Thursday in July and again at Assumptiontide (15th August and the following Sunday).

Northamptonshire

Broughton Tin Can Band, formed in the middle ages to cast out gypsies, may still be heard once a year. The performance commences at midnight on the second Sunday after St Andrew's Day, 30th November. A group of about sixty players marches through the streets banging on tin cans and buckets, and this cacophony lasts for about an hour.

The Pole Fair, or Charter Fair, takes place every twenty years at **Corby** on Spring Bank Holiday Monday. The next is due in 2002.

At **Flore** near Weedon the May Day celebrations are held on either the first or the second Saturday after 1st May and are led by the Church of England Primary School. A May garland is paraded round the village before the crowning of the May Queen in the afternoon.

Oak Apple Day (29th May) is marked in **Northampton** by the placing of a wreath of oak leaves on the statue of Charles II in All Saints' church. This commemorates the king's gift of wood to the town for rebuilding, after most of it had been destroyed in a great fire in 1675.

On Ascension Day the people of **Wicken** celebrate the unification of two parishes in 1587 with a Love Feast held on the lawn of the old rectory, which is now an hotel. After a short church service they process to the grounds, where they sing the Old Hundredth psalm before the feast of cakes and ale.

Northumberland

At **Allendale** the New Year is welcomed in spectacular fashion by men in fancy dress who process through the streets carrying containers of burning tar on their heads. The barrels are thrown on an unlit bonfire just before midnight to ignite it, and as midnight strikes all present dance round singing 'Auld Lang Syne'. Then the men go first-footing in the traditional way.

Alnwick on Shrove Tuesday is the scene of a game of Shrovetide football. The game, between the parishes of St Michael and St Paul, now takes place in a field, although it used to be played through the streets. The ball is piped on to the pitch by the Duke of Northumberland's piper, and kick-off is at 2.30 p.m. The goals are a quarter of a mile (400 metres) apart, and the teams may contain over 150 people. The ball may not be handled. After three goals have been scored the game ceases; the ball is thrown in the air, and

The Alnwick ball game takes place at the Northumberland town every Shrove Tuesday.

the person who succeeds in carrying it off the pitch retains it.

The historic town of **Berwick-upon-Tweed** maintains several old traditions. Curfew is rung each night, except Sunday, at 8 p.m., and the Pancake Bell is rung on Shrove Tuesday. The mayor and other officials perambulate the boundaries on horseback annually on May Day; parts of the boundary inspected include some of the border between Scotland and England. In 1945 the custom of Crowning the Salmon Queen was revived at nearby Tweedmouth.

Several traditional bells are rung at **Morpeth**, including curfew nightly at 8 p.m. and the market bell on Wednesdays. The Riding of the Borough Boundaries takes place on the Thursday nearest 25th April and can attract up to two hundred riders. This event used to take place on St Mark's Day (25th April) and was fol- lowed by races in which the burgesses competed for a piece of plate given by the magistrates. The Morpeth Gathering takes place on the weekend after Easter; running from the Friday to the Sunday, it includes various traditional sports as well as music and dancing.

The Walking of the Bounds at **Newbiggin-by-the-Sea** has been practised since 1235 and now takes place annually on the Wednes- day nearest 18th May. During the walk new freeholders are initi- ated by allowing themselves to be bumped three times on a bound- ary stone known as the Dunting Stone on Newbiggin Moor. Nuts and raisins are scattered after the ceremony.

A modern custom, instituted in 1955, is the annual presentation of a red rose to the Duke of Northumberland or his agent as token rent for a piece of land near the church at **Newburn**. The rent for this land, used as an open space, is paid in August.

On Dookie Apple Night (Hallowe'en – 31st October) in **New- castle upon Tyne** children parade through the streets carrying the traditional turnip lanterns. Also in Newcastle, every seventh year during September is held the traditional auction of leases of the intakes of the Town Moor, by the sand-glass method.

The Rogation Ceremony at **North Shields**, which used to be held on the fifth Sunday after Easter, now takes place at the late Spring Bank Holiday. After an open-air service on the quay, the clergy and choir travel down the river Tyne, along the border between North Shields and South Shields, blessing the boats.

On 14th February on Pedwell Beach at **Norham** the vicar blesses the nets at the opening of the salmon-fishing season. All present repeat the ancient Pedwell Prayer, and the first net is cast and drawn. The officiating priest receives the first salmon caught.

On 5th July, Old Midsummer's Eve, at **Whalton**, near Morpeth, a bonfire, known as the Bale or Baal Fire, is lit on the village green, accompanied by music and dancing. In olden times villagers used

The Rocking Ceremony at Blidworth in Nottinghamshire symbolises the presentation of the young Jesus at the temple.

to leap through the flames; nowadays children dance round, and sweets are distributed.

Nottinghamshire

At the church of St Mary, **Blidworth**, an event believed to be unique in England takes place on the Sunday nearest 2nd February (the Feast of the Purification of the Blessed Virgin Mary). Known as the Rocking Ceremony, it was revived by the vicar in 1922 and symbolises the presentation of the young Jesus at the temple. The most recently baptised male child in the parish, carried by his parents and attended by his godparents, is formally presented to the priest, who places him in a cradle before the altar. In the course of a short service of dedication the flower-bedecked cradle is rocked by the priest several times before the child is handed back to his parents while the Nunc Dimittis is sung.

On 6th December, St Nicholas's Day, a boy bishop (or child

bishop) is enthroned at **Edwinstowe**.

Laxton is the only English village where the ancient open-field system of farming has survived practically unchanged since the Norman conquest. Agricultural matters are governed by the Court Leet, which meets annually in December. A jury appointed by the court carries out an inspection of the winter cornfield every November to ensure that everything is in order. Fines for mismanagement are collected at the court meeting.

The annual Gopher Ringing at **Newark** commemorates a Flemish merchant named Gopher who became lost in the marshes round the town but was guided to safety by the Newark bells. He left some money for the church bells to be rung on the five Sundays before Christmas. On Shrove Tuesday the Pancake Bell is rung from Newark parish church.

The Hercules Clay Commemoration Service takes place at the parish church of St Mary Magdalene in **Newark** in March. Hercules Clay, a Royalist, was mayor of Newark in 1643, during the Civil War. One night he dreamt that his house was on fire; taking this to be a divine warning, he moved his family out. The next day his house was hit by a Cromwellian cannonball, which set it alight. He died the following year and, in thankfulness for his family's escape, left a legacy providing for an annual sermon 'to exhort the people not to set their affections on things of this world but by their

The maypole is permanently raised at Wellow, Nottinghamshire.

good works to lay hold on eternal life'. He also allowed money for bread to be distributed to the poor. Today the sermon is part of the activities of the Newark Chamber of Trade. Loaves are distributed to the choirboys after the service.

Nottingham Goose Fair, the biggest fair in Britain, takes place on the last three days of the first week of October.

Records of maypole dancing at **Wellow** (now held on Spring Bank Holiday Monday) extend back to the beginning of the nineteenth century. The 65 foot (20 metre) maypole, topped by its golden weathercock and vane, is a permanent feature of the village green.

Oxfordshire

At **Abingdon**, in addition to the election of the Mayor of Ock Street on the Saturday after 19th June, the custom of bun throwing by the mayor and corporation is still maintained. Buns similar to hot cross buns are thrown from the top of County Hall to people assembled in the Market Place. There is much competition to obtain a bun, and some families have a complete collection of buns from every throwing since the coronation of George III, when the custom originated. Bun throwing takes place on occasions of special importance to the town.

The Great Shirt Race at **Bampton**, which takes place towards the end of May, was started in 1953 to celebrate the coronation of Elizabeth II. That first race was for adults only, and nurses from the Oxford hospitals were invited to make a collection during the race. Over the years the event has evolved so that there are separate races for the primary and secondary school children. The event includes a fancy dress parade, and a collection is made for the benefit of local pensioners. However, Bampton is a guardian of far older traditions. It is most famous for its morris-dance tradition, said to go back several hundred years. The Bampton Morris Men make their appearance on the Spring Bank Holiday, when the dancers are accompanied by a sword-bearer. The cake he distributes to the onlookers is said to bring good luck and husbands for the girls. The Spring Bank Holiday Monday is also Garland Day, when the children parade garlands of flowers around the village. The village mummers' play was revived in 1946 and is performed around the village on Christmas Eve.

In the church at **Charlton-on-Otmoor** a cross covered with box branches, known locally as the May Garland, stands on the screen throughout the year. The greenery is renewed for May Day and for the dedication festival in September. At 9 a.m. on May Day, or on the nearest schoolday, the children walk from the school to the church carrying a long garland decorated with leaves and flowers. Each child also makes and brings a small cross decorated with flowers; before they enter the church they sing the May Garland Song. In church the garland is hung on the screen, there is a short service, and the two best crosses are hung over the church door, to be left until they fade. Before they return to school the children dance in the streets outside the church. Before 1963 the children used to carry their small crosses from house to house singing a little song and asking for pennies.

Headington Quarry, on the east side of Oxford, is noted for its long morris-dancing tradition; the dancers make their appearance on Spring Bank Holiday Monday. It was the Headington Quarry side's unseasonable performance on Boxing Day 1899, to raise extra cash for the dancers, that first brought morris dancing to the attention of Cecil Sharp. This led to the founding of the English Folk Dance Society in 1911 and the subsequent revival in traditional dance. At Christmas the traditional mumming play is still performed.

The fair on Trinity Monday at **Kirtlington** is the last vestige of the Lamb-ale suppressed in 1858.

Several old customs are preserved at **Oxford**. After dinner on New Year's Day the bursar of Queen's College presents every fellow with a needle and coloured thread, saying 'Take it and be thrifty', thus fulfilling the terms of an old bequest.

On Ascension Day after a service in St Michael's church the bounds of the parish are beaten. Choirboys and others who assist in the ceremonies receive hot pennies after a traditional lunch at Lincoln College.

St Giles Fair is held in the city centre on the Monday and Tuesday of the first complete week of September.

The Hymn of Thanksgiving, *Te Deum Patrem Collimus*, written about 1600, is always included among the May Day carols which are sung from the top of Magdalen College Tower at 6 a.m. on 1st May. After the singing the college bells ring out, and there is morris dancing in the High Street. On the Sunday after St John the Baptist's Day (24th June) the Wall Pulpit Sermon is preached from an open-air pulpit in the first quadrangle at Magdalen College, commemorating the fact that a hospital of St John the Baptist once stood on the site. The Simon Perrot Oration is given on the first Monday of the Trinity Term at Magdalen College.

At the Boar's Head Ceremony at Queen's College in December a boar's head is carried in as part of the Christmas fare. The Provost, dons and fellows are summoned by blowing an ancient hunting horn, and as the head is carried in the traditional carol is sung in Latin.

On 23rd April the Shakespeare Memorial Ceremony takes place.

The mayor and civic officials go in procession to the Painted Room in the Cornmarket, Oxford, and drink the poet's health in sack and malmsey. This room was once the property of New College and was called the Crown Tavern. The landlord was John Davenant, later mayor of Oxford, and the father of the poet Sir William Davenant, Shakespeare's godson. The family were close friends of Shakespeare, and Aubrey recorded that Shakespeare often stayed here on the journey between Stratford-upon-Avon and London.

In 1965, after a lapse of about two hundred years, there was a revival of Clipping the Church at **Radley** on Easter Sunday.

At **Shenington** near Banbury grass is strewn in Holy Trinity church annually on Whit Saturday and renewed the following Saturday.

An apprentice bell is tolled daily at 6 a.m. and the curfew nightly at 9 p.m. at **Wallingford**. The latter is said to have originated in the time of William I, who granted Wallingford a later curfew than that imposed upon the rest of England because the town allowed him unimpeded passage when he crossed the Thames there on his way from Hastings to London.

Rutland

On St Peter's Day (29th June) rushes are spread on the floor of the church at **Barrowden**. Certain fields were bequeathed to the church many years ago, so that their rents would pay for the upkeep of the church. The tenant is required to provide rushes for spreading on

the church floor on St Peter's Day, or else his tenancy is forfeit. Recently some of the ceremonies which attach to this custom elsewhere, notably in the Lake District, were revived here.

Hay is scattered on the floor of the church at **Langham** on the patronal feast day of St Peter and St Paul (towards the end of June). The hay is scattered on

Part of the horseshoe collection at Oakham Castle.

Children dressed in eighteenth-century costume celebrate Arbor Day at Aston-on-Clun.

the day before (a Saturday), when the church is decorated. This custom is said to commemorate the gratitude of a traveller who lost his way one winter night and was saved by the ringing of Langham church bells. Until the mid nineteenth century the hay came from a field known as Bell Acre, which was left to the church on condition that hay from it was scattered on the church floor every year.

The first time any peer of the realm passes through **Oakham** he is required to present a horseshoe, or the money to have one made, to the lord of the manor. There is a remarkable collection of these shoes in the castle, including one purporting to have been left by Elizabeth I and one presented by the present Queen in 1967.

Shropshire

A tree in the centre of **Aston-on-Clun** is decorated the year round with flags. These are changed on 29th May, known locally as Arbor Day. According to legend, when the lord of the manor, John Marston, brought his new bride, Mary Carter, home to the village on 29th May 1789 she was delighted to see the tree decorated with flags, believing them to have been put up in her honour. She insisted that the Marston family pay for the annual replacement of the flags, which they did until 1951. The parish council then took over the responsibility for replacing the flags. A fund-raising fete is held on a Sunday near to Arbor Day, during which children in period costume re-enact the arrival of John and Mary Marston at the village. It is probable that Mary saw an already established custom and mistakenly thought the flags were put up in her honour.

Somerset

Guy Fawkes Carnival at **Bridgwater** claims an unbroken record since 1605. When the news of the failure of the Gunpowder Plot reached the town, bonfires were lit and impromptu processions were held, and the celebrations have been repeated annually ever since, except during the war years. Nowadays the carnival is held on the nearest Thursday to 5th November.

On 17th January (Old Twelfth Night) **Carhampton** is the scene of a centuries-old custom known as Wassailing the Apple Trees. In order to safeguard the trees and drive away any evil spirits which might harm the apple crops, villagers encircle the largest tree in one of the local orchards. The branches are decorated with toast soaked in cider, an incantation is sung, cider is thrown on to the tree, and guns are fired into its branches. Then the tree is toasted in cider, and a song, urging it to bear much fruit, is sung. Apple wassailing has been reintroduced at **Norton Fitzwarren** near Taunton; this is a private affair (by invitation only) and is sponsored by a cider producer.

The **Chedzoy** candle auction is held every twenty-one years. The next is due in the year 2009. An acre of land (0.4 hectare) was donated to the church in 1490 for auction every twenty-one years to raise money for church repairs. The bidding is started when the auctioneer lights a half-inch (13 mm) candle, and the winning bid is the last before the flame expires.

An old custom which has been revived at a **Dunster** hotel is the Burning of the Ashen Faggot on Christmas Eve. The faggot of ash twigs, bound with green ash bands, is burned on an open fire, and as each band bursts a round of cider is drunk. Some of the charred remains are retained to ignite the next year's faggot.

The Cheese Show at **Frome**, which began in 1877, arising out of the Frome Fair, is organised by the Frome District Agricultural Society on the last Wednesday in September. During the day the competing cheeses are rolled down to the river and dunked in the water.

At the historic town of **Glastonbury** the Holy Thorn, said to be a descendant of the tree which sprang from a thorn staff plunged into the ground by Joseph of Arimathea, is reputed to flower on Old Christmas Day (6th January). In fact it may flower at any time in late December or early January, and many people visit the town to see this. It is customary for some sprays to be cut from the tree a few days before Christmas by the mayor and the vicar of the church of St John the Baptist for dispatch to the Queen.

The last Thursday of October is Punky Night at **Hinton St George**. Children carve the traditional Hallowe'en lanterns, known here as 'punkies', from mangel-wurzels and go through the streets singing; when they knock on doors they receive either money or a candle from the householders. The custom is said to have originated when the women of the village had to go out on the night of the nearby Chiselborough fair to find and bring home their drunken husbands, carrying 'punkies' to light their way.

Minehead Hobby Horse appears on the streets on the evening of 30th April, known as Warning Eve, on May Day itself and on the following two days. The Hobby Horse is a structure resembling a bearded horse, over 6 feet (1.8 metres) long, with a boat-shaped body made of canvas and decorated with ribbons. It may represent a survival of ancient fertility rites but is also said to recall a shipwreck on May Day Eve 1722, when a cow was washed ashore; its tail was cut off, attached to a hobby horse and used to chastise people who caused displeasure.

The ancient Shrovetide custom of Egg Shackling survives in the villages of **Stoke St Gregory** and **Shepton Beauchamp**, where the children take eggs to school on Shrove Tuesday. The eggs are marked with the child's name and gently shaken together in a sieve. At Stoke St Gregory this takes place in school in the morning and at Shepton Beauchamp in the afternoon. At both schools prizes are awarded to the owners of the longest surviving eggs; at Shepton Beauchamp the last three win small amounts of money, left by a local benefactor. It is believed that the origin of the custom is to get rid of the eggs before the Lenten fast. However, another story says that at one time the eggs were given to the vicar to ensure that he would not starve during the forty meatless days of Lent.

At the **Tatworth** candle auction, held annually on the Tuesday following the first Saturday after 6th April, a piece of land known as Stowell Meadow is let. During the proceedings, at which an inch (25 mm) of candle is used, no one may rise from his seat or speak except to bid, and the last bid before the candle goes out is the successful one. No pin is used in this case, as it is in other candle auctions.

Staffordshire

On the Monday following 4th September **Abbots Bromley** is the scene of the famous Horn Dance, which commemorates the granting to the villagers of hunting rights in Needwood Forest. Ancient reindeer horns set into wooden 'heads' are carried by dancers dressed in Tudor-style costumes. The costumes were designed and first made by the daughters of the then vicar in about 1860; previously the dancers had worn their everyday clothes. They dance thoughout the day in the locality of the village, accompanied by traditional figures such as Maid Marian, Robin Hood and a hobby horse, but the horns are never allowed to leave the parish.

One of the few places outside Derbyshire where there is a well-dressing is **Endon**. It has taken place since 1845, and the crowning of a well-dressing queen dates from 1868. The event occurs over Spring Bank Holiday Weekend.

The sole warden of **Leek** parish church also holds the ancient office of Warden of Leek. Three nominations for this appointment are made at the annual vestry, held usually in April in one of

The Sheriff's Ride at Lichfield in Staffordshire follows the boundaries of the city.

70

the churches in Leek. All ratepayers may attend, and any rate-payer may be nominated. If there are more than three nominations a town election is held.

Lichfield has maintained several ancient customs. At noon on St George's Day (23rd April) the Court of View of Frank Pledge and the Court Baron of the Burgesses, otherwise St George's Court, are held in the Guildhall. The town clerk, as steward of the manor, presides, and a jury is present to hear complaints and to appoint two high constables, a bailiff and other officers.

On Ascension Day the ecclesiastical bounds are beaten by cathedral officials. The procession of choir and clergy carries elm boughs and stops at eight places to sing a psalm. On their return to the cathedral the boughs are placed round the font.

On Spring Bank Holiday Monday the Court of Arraye and Court Leet are held. Youths in ancient coats of mail parade for inspection by town officials. This custom dates from times when freemen were required to have suits of armour and weapons ready for use in war, and these were inspected annually. On the same day the Greenhill Bower takes place; this probably started as a pagan floral rite, and in the middle ages various craft guilds used to parade. Today there is a floral procession and a fair.

The Riding of the City Bounds of Lichfield used to take place in the spring, but under a charter granted by Queen Mary in 1553 the sheriff had to ride the bounds on the feast of the Nativity of the Virgin Mary, 8th September; today it usually takes place on the nearest Saturday. Various halts for refreshment are made on the 24 mile (39 km) ride.

On the Saturday nearest 18th September the mayor, sheriff, members of the Johnson Society and boys from the King Edward VI School walk in procession from the Guildhall to the Market Place, where a wreath is laid on Dr Samuel Johnson's statue to commemorate his birthday. At a commemorative supper in the evening Johnson's favourite meal, steak and kidney pie and apple tart with cream, is served. On 21st December, St Thomas's Day, every house in the Cathedral Close receives one small loaf provided by the dean's vicar.

Uttoxeter also remembers Dr Johnson's birthday. On the Monday following the Lichfield ceremony, a wreath is fixed to a plaque on the wall of an old stone kiosk in the Market Place. This commemorates an occasion when Johnson, whose father kept a bookstall in the market, stood in the rain there as an act of penance for disobeying an order from his father in his youth. On Christmas Eve Guizers perform a mumming play in public houses around Uttoxeter; on Christmas Day they perform in private houses.

Suffolk

The Cakes and Ale Ceremony at **Bury St Edmunds** commemorates the town's great benefactor, Jankyn Smith. In June the almshouse residents attend a service at St Mary's church, at which the oldest endowed sermon in England is preached. This is followed by a meal for the tenants and trustees at the Guildhall. In the past the tenants (known as licensees) received alms of one shilling (5p) after the service.

On Easter Monday the Race of the Bogmen and egg-throwing take place outside the Chestnut Horse at **Great Finborough**.

A boy bishop is annually enthroned at Mendlesham in Suffolk.

Originally the winner of the race, first held in 1896, gained a contract to plough and sow the land of a nearby farm. The event fell into abeyance in 1915 but was revived in the 1970s, supplemented by egg-throwing outside the pub after the race.

On the Sunday nearest St Nicholas's Day a boy bishop is enthroned at **Mendlesham**. This ceremony was instigated in 1981.

Trinity Fair, **Southwold**, begins on the first Monday of June and lasts for three days. The fair is opened by the mayor, who then takes a ride on the dodgems (the other civic dignitaries usually take a ride on rival dodgems), before attending the Trinity Lunch. Before the opening of the fair the mayor visits the local primary school and distributes Trinity Money (50p) to the children.

The distribution of Carlow Bread takes place at **Woodbridge** on 2nd February. George Carlow, a local tanner, died in 1783 and was buried in his garden. He left a rent charge of one pound on the property to provide sixty twopenny loaves and six score penny loaves for distribution to the poor on Candlemas Day forever. About twenty loaves are handed out today at his tomb, which is situated in the grounds of the Bull Hotel, the owner of which pays the rental.

Surrey

The foundation stone of the almshouses at **Croydon** was laid on 22nd March 1618, and ever since then a Founder's Day service has been held each year at Croydon parish church, usually on 22nd March. It commemorates Archbishop Whitgift, the founder, and is attended by the residents of the almshouses and Whitgift House, representatives of the three schools run by the Whitgift Foundation and members of the Fishmongers' Company. A wreath is laid on Whitgift's tomb. This is not a public event.

A ceremony held annually in the Guildhall, **Guildford**, at the end of January or beginning of February is known as Dicing for the Maids' Money. Under the will of John How, dated 1674, two long-serving maids within the borough of Guildford cast dice for the interest on £400 left for this purpose; this amounts to about £12. Under another charity dating from 1704 there is a larger income originally intended for an impoverished apprentice within the borough. Since no one seems to qualify nowadays under the original terms of the second will, the trustees give this money to the runner-up at dice, who therefore benefits more than the winner.

Mitcham Fair is held over three days in mid August. Despite a 'charter key' that symbolically opens the fair, it was never actually granted a charter.

On 12th August at **Sutton** Mary Gibson's tomb is ceremonially examined. Mary Gibson apparently had a fear of premature burial and left a legacy to allow for an annual inspection of her tomb.

Yet another bequest governs the curious events which occasionally take place in the churchyard at **Wotton** near Dorking on 2nd February. William Glanville, who was buried here in 1711, left £2 to each of five boys of the parish under sixteen years of age provided that they recite the Ten Commandments, the Apostles' Creed and the Lord's Prayer with their hands resting on his tomb. They must also read and write a portion of one of St Paul's Epistles to the Corinthians. The two boys who gain the highest marks in the competition for these awards receive an additional reward if they are willing to be apprenticed to a trade.

Sussex (East)

Good Friday skipping, a custom once common in Sussex and believed to make the crops grow, now survives only at the Rose Cottage inn, **Alciston**, where people skip on Good Friday morning using a long rope provided by the landlord. At **Brighton** this day was known as Long Rope Day until about 1850, an acknowledgement of the practise of this custom by the fisherfolk on the beach.

An old-established marbles match takes place at **Battle** on Good Friday against nearby Netherfield, and there is a distribution of hot cross buns.

There is a pancake race at **Bodiam** on Shrove Tuesday.

At **Hastings** daily at 6.30 a.m. there is a 'Dutch auction' in the fish market; the auctioneer names a higher price than he expects to obtain for the day's catch and gradually reduces it. The first person to make a bid gets the fish.

On the Wednesday before Ascension Day (sometime in May) the rectors of All Saints' and St Clement's churches in **Hastings** conduct a service on the foreshore at which the Blessing of the Sea takes place. The procession begins at 7 p.m.

Since 1897 an annual pilgrimage has been made from the church of St Mary Star of the Sea to the ruins of the Chapel of Our Lady in **Hastings** Castle for the celebration of mass; this usually occurs on the last Sunday in July.

The title of Champion Town Crier of England is awarded after an annual contest that takes place in **Hastings** in August. All the contestants, many of whom wear magnificent uniforms, read the same 150-word text, following the customary cries of 'Oyez, oyez'.

In October an eight-day celebration of **Hastings** takes place. The genesis of the event was in 1966, when the nine-hundredth anniversary of the foundation of the town was celebrated. In 1968 the

The famous 5th November celebrations at Lewes in Sussex.

first Hastings Day was organised, and this has since become an annual event lasting eight days, with music, sports and flag ceremonies. All the organisations in the town contribute to the event. A recent addition to Hastings Day is the revival by Hastings Borough Bonfire Society of the bonfire tradition in Hastings; a torchlight procession culminates in a bonfire and fireworks display, featuring the 'largest Guy Fawkes in England' on the Saturday nearest 14th October.

Another revival in **Hastings**, since 1982, has been the Jack-in-the-Green procession through the Old Town on May Day, with morris dancers from all over England. In the nineteenth century this was a chimney-sweeps' procession.

At **Lewes** 5th November is celebrated with torchlight processions, the burning of effigies, firework displays and the rolling of lighted tar barrels down the street. All this commemorates the martyrdom of seventeen local people, burned at the stake in the reign of Mary Tudor, as well as Guy Fawkes. The events are organised by several bonfire societies.

Guy Fawkes celebrations at **Rye** include the burning of a boat on the Saltings, recalling the burning of captured boats by the towns-people when the French used to raid the town. Here, on Mayoring Day, towards the end of May, the mayor and other council officials throw hot pennies from the town-hall windows at noon to children in the street.

Sussex (West)

On the first Monday of May the May Queen, chosen from the Youth Group of the Chichester Folk Dance Club, is crowned at the City Cross in **Chichester**. Afterwards there is folk and morris dancing in the street by members of the Chichester Folk Dance Club and the Martlet Sword and Morris Men.

The **Ebernoe** Horn Fair on 25th July is now a funfair, but during the day there is also a cricket match, and a whole black ram is roasted in a pit. At the mutton supper which follows the match the batsman with the highest score is presented with the ram's head and horns.

There is an early start to the **Shoreham-by-Sea** May Day celebrations. Members of the Shoreham Folk Dance Club and the Sompting Village Morris meet around 6 a.m. and dance in the street outside St Mary's Hall, East Street. They process usually to the old people's home near the community centre, where they crown the May Queen at 7.00 to 7.30 a.m. She is usually an adult member of the dance club. They dance again in honour of the May Queen before processing back to St Mary's Hall, where they disperse.

Every Good Friday the British Individual Marbles Champion-ship is held at **Tinsley Green** near Crawley. About the year 1600 two rivals are supposed to have competed at marbles for the hand of a local beauty. Nowadays it is a highly organised team com-petition played under strict rules, and the two players with the highest scores compete for the individual title.

Warwickshire

A Court Leet is held annually at **Alcester**.

The **Atherstone** Shrove Tuesday football game, played with a water-filled ball decorated with the colours of the local football team, lasts only two hours after kick-off at 3 p.m. The game originated in the reign of King John as a contest between men from Warwickshire and Leicestershire for a bag of gold.

The **Coventry** Mystery Plays are performed every two or three years in the ruins of the old cathedral. The last performance was in 1997. It is advisable to contact the tourist informtion office for details of the next performance.

The lord of the manor, the Duke of Buccleuch, or his agent collects yearly tithes from representatives of various surrounding parishes at **Knightlow Hill** before dawn on the morning of 11th November, St Martin's Day. After the reading of the Charter of Assembly, each person throws his money, known as Wroth Silver, into the stone base of an old cross. This payment preserves a right to drive cattle across the Duke's land, and the penalty for non-payment is a pound for every penny owed. Breakfast is then taken at a local inn.

The Cyclists' War Memorial at **Meriden** was unveiled on 21st May 1921, and a remembrance service, attended by cyclists from all over England, has been held there annually since then on the nearest Sunday to this date.

The archery meetings of the Woodmen of Arden are also held at **Meriden**; the most important one, known as the Grand Wardmote, occurs in July. The Woodmen wear a distinctive uniform of green hats, buff waistcoats and white breeches. Their records date only from 1785, although it is said that Robin Hood competed here.

The Shakespeare Birthday Celebrations at **Stratford-upon-Avon** on the Saturday nearest 23rd April make a colourful occasion with flags of many nations flying from decorated poles down the centre of Bridge Street; a procession of townspeople and visitors wends its way to Shakespeare's grave to lay wreaths.

The Mop Fair at **Stratford-upon-Avon** is now a huge funfair, but it was originally a hiring fair held on 12th October. A week after the Friday following the Mop Fair there is another fair, known as the 'Runaway Mop', which provided those who were not happy with the employment obtained at the Mop Fair with a chance to find a new employer. This too is now a funfair although not as big as the earlier fair.

The first Ascension Day Tower Service was held in **Warwick** in 1907 on the tower of St Mary's church. Today it is no longer a service as such, but from 7 a.m. the three Anglican church choirs in the town sing from the three church towers in turn to a planned timetable.

A meeting of **Warwick** Court Leet is held annually on the last Thursday in October. It still possesses certain powers concerning St Mary's Common and appoints four chamberlains to control matters connected with this land. Bread-weighers, ale-tasters, fish- and flesh-tasters, butter-weighers and overseers of pavements, with purely nominal duties, are also appointed.

There is a permanent maypole on the village green at **Welford-on-Avon**, where maypole dancing has taken place since the end of the nineteenth century at least. It usually occurs on the second or third Saturday afternoon in May.

Wiltshire

The two-hundred-year-old annual dinner for 'threshers and labourers', known as the Duck Feast, is held at **Charlton St Peter**, near Upavon, to commemorate the Reverend Stephen Duck, who was born here and became known as the Thresher Poet.

Great Wishford near Salisbury maintains two old customs. On Rogation Monday the annual sale of Midsummer Tithes takes place. This is a sale of grazing rights on 6.5 acres (2.6 hectares) of church land and is conducted by the parish clerk or churchwarden in the churchyard just before sunset. With the church key in his hand, the official walks between the church porch and the gate, inviting bids. Bidding continues until the sun sinks below the horizon; as soon as it has disappeared he strikes the gate with the key, and the rights go to the last person to bid before this occurs.

In 1603 the villagers of **Great Wishford** were granted the right to gather wood for all time in Grovely Forest, and they confirm this privilege by marching once a year on 29th May to the forest to cut wood. They return to the village with large branches and process through the streets carrying a banner bearing the words 'Grovely, Grovely, and all Grovely! Unity is Strength', and shouting the words 'Grovely, Grovely and all Grovely'.

The annual Tayler Charity Service on the Wednesday of Easter week at **Keevil** church is followed by a distribution of buns. Under the terms of this bequest, a 'sermon is to be preached suited to the capacity of children and young persons', after which a fourpenny cake must be provided for each teacher present and a twopenny cake for each scholar. Nowadays the cakes provided cost more than this!

Malmesbury Old Corporation Courts are held four times a year: at Trinity, on King Athelstan's Feast Day a week afterwards, at Michaelmas, and on 31st December. These meetings, held in the

Villagers at Great Wishford, Wiltshire, restate their rights to Grovely Forest.

Courthouse of St John, near St John's Bridge, are superintended by the High Steward or the Warden and attended by the assistant burgesses, landholders and commoners. A grant of land was made to the people of the town by King Athelstan in 930, and various persons are still entitled to a plot, claims for which must be made at the court.

The Companions of the Most Ancient Order of Druids keep a midnight vigil on 21st June at **Stonehenge** and hold their summer solstice service as the sun shines directly over the altar stone at dawn. A second service is held at noon. Hundreds of people watch this event.

Worcestershire

On the last Saturday in June the **Bromsgrove** Court Leet begins with a parade of the court bailiff and officers in full regalia.

The four-hundred-year-old Winbury Dole distribution takes place after morning service on New Year's Day at **Castlemorton**, when cake is distributed. The fund of ten shillings *per annum* derives from a charge on a field near Druggers Lane End.

Another bequest provides for the **Kidderminster** Feast of Peace and Good Neighbourhood, which still takes place annually. It originated in the fifteenth century when an unknown maiden lady left a bequest of forty shillings to the inhabitants of Church Street 'to be put out to interest to provide farthing loaves for the people of the street' and to enable the men to meet once a year to settle their differences peaceably. Three hundred years later a further £150 was bequeathed to provide plum cake, pipes, tobacco and ale for the men at their midsummer gathering. Church Street is now a professional and business area of the town, but the Feast is continued, with a different person or company each year playing host. The event has two parts: the distribution of the 'farthing loaves and twopenny plum cakes' (supplied by the same local baker since the mid nineteenth century); and the Midsummer Eve supper in St Mary's Chantry, attended by the mayor, when long-stemmed clay pipes (known as the 'pipes of peace') are smoked.

Oak Apple day is celebrated in **Worcester** by decorating the gates of the Guildhall with oak branches.

Yorkshire (East)

At **Market Weighton** a horse race that is said to be the oldest in England, if not in the world, takes place on the third Thursday in March. The Kiplingcotes Derby, which has been held every year since 1519, is run over a 4 mile (6.4 km) course, passing through five parishes and finishing near Kiplingcotes Farm. Riders, who must be over 10 stone (63 kg) in weight, are weighed on a coal merchant's scale. The prize money for second place is larger than that for the winner.

Yorkshire (North)

From Michaelmas until Shrove Tuesday a horn is sounded nightly at 10 o'clock on **Bainbridge** village green; this custom is over seven hundred years old.

On the first Tuesday in August the **Egton Bridge** Gooseberry Society holds its annual Gooseberry Contest at the village school. Established in 1800, this is England's oldest gooseberry show.

On the Saturday after 6th January the long-sword dance teams at **Goathland**, about 7 miles (11 km) south of Whitby, perform their sword dance around the village. At one time the dancers, known as the Plough Stots, would drag a plough with them; now they simply have it blessed in church on the previous Sunday (Plough Sunday).

On the first Monday of the year a candle auction for a 16 acre

(6.5 hectare) piece of land known as Poor's Pasture takes place at **Hubberholme**. Only a few visitors are allowed to attend the auction, which finishes when a pin stuck into a burning candle falls.

Several customs are still observed at **Richmond**. The Apprentice and Curfew Bells are rung at 8 a.m. and 8 p.m. respectively; the Pancake Bell is rung on Shrove Tuesday, and the Passing Bell as appropriate. Every year, on a variable date in September (usually the first Saturday), the mayor, as Clerk of the Market, presents a bottle of wine to the first local farmer who brings to the market cross a 'respectable sample of the new season's wheat', the First

The Curfew Horn is blown each evening at 9 p.m. in Ripon market place.

Fruits of the Harvest. This wine is used to drink the mayor's health, and the farmer receives a second bottle to take home. Every seventh year the bounds are beaten. The mayor and various officials make a 15 mile (24 km) circuit of the boundary. This used to include a wade in the river Swale, but this wet task is now performed by only one person, the Water Wader. New pennies are distributed during the perambulation.

The Curfew Horn is sounded each evening at 9 p.m. in the market place at **Ripon**; the horn makes five additional appearances through the year, on 'Horn Days', when the Hornblower leads a procession of the civic dignitaries to the cathedral, notably on St Wilfrid's Sunday (the first Sunday of August). On Boxing Day in Ripon a 'sword dance play' is performed around the pubs and streets. The play is a mumming play that may have been associated with a sword dance; however, dancing no longer features in the performance.

The Shrove Tuesday Pancake Bell is rung in **Scarborough**, and Shrovetide skipping (a relic of an old Shrovetide fair) takes place on the foreshore in the afternoon, when all who wish may skip, using long ropes provided for the purpose.

Beating the bounds of the manor of **Spaunton** involves a 30 mile (48 km) hike and takes place only occasionally, when a new lord of the manor takes over the estate.

The Burning of Bartle has taken place at **West Witton** for many years and now occurs on the evening of the Saturday nearest St Bartholomew's Day in August. Old Bartle was probably a local villain who persistently stole the villagers' swine; when they chased him down the local fellside towards the village he fell and broke his neck and was finally burnt at the stake in Grassgill Lane. An effigy of Old Bartle is made in great secrecy and carried through the village after dark. The procession stops at intervals to shout a verse relating the fate of Old Bartle during the chase, and the dummy is finally consigned to the flames in Grassgill Lane.

A Shrove Tuesday Pancake Race, apparently a revival of an old tradition, takes place on the West Pier at **Whitby**; the winner receives a cup. There is a Rogationtide Blessing of the Sea in May, and on the morning of the day before Ascension Day the Planting of the Penny Hedge takes place. The story relates that when a hermit gave refuge to a wild boar the angry huntsmen broke into his cell and attacked him. As he died he begged the Abbot of Whitby to show mercy to his attackers if they and their descendants would do penance. They were ordered to erect a hedge of stakes and branches at the water's edge each year, strong enough to resist the onslaught of three tides. This hedge is still planted every year.

The famous **York** Mystery Plays originated about 1350 and are now performed triennially in June in the ruins of St Mary's Abbey.

Shovetide skipping at Scarborough, North Yorkshire.

The ringing of the Curfew Bell at St Michael's church, Spurriergate, which ceased in about 1931, has been revived, and a new curfew bell, which can be rung automatically, was installed in 1987.

Yorkshire (South)

The Longsword Dancers at **Grenoside** and **Handsworth** (north and east of Sheffield respectively) make their appearance on Boxing Day.

In the area around **Sheffield** there are some customs associated with public houses. On 30th October (or within a few days) there is a custom where men put on disguises and others in the pub have to guess who they are. From mid November until Christmas there is carol singing in many of the pubs; the carols, however, are not the ones generally heard and sung in churches at this period.

Yorkshire (West)

Three 'pole men', elected by the villagers, supervise the lowering of the maypole, said to be the tallest in England, at **Barwick-in-Elmet** every third year on Easter Monday, so that it can be repainted. Maypole Raising Day on Spring Bank Holiday is celebrated with sports, processions and music. The next lowering of the maypole should occur in 1999.

The Pace Egg Play at **Brighouse** has been performed annually on Easter Saturday since 1949. The performers are members of the Brighouse Children's Theatre, which was founded in 1948. Although there had been a local Pace Egg play the text had been lost, so the published text from Midgley was used in this revival.

The first **Denby Dale** pie was baked in 1788, and six have been made since then to mark various notable events; one was made in 1964 to celebrate the birth of four royal babies in one year. The huge pie was cut up, and pieces were sold for charity.

At **Dewsbury** on Christmas Eve the Devil's Knell is tolled. Beginning at 11 p.m., one stroke is tolled for every year since the birth of Christ, the holy birth heralding the Devil's demise.

The May Day celebrations at **Gawthorpe** include all the traditional events: the crowning of the May Queen, a spectacular procession and morris dancing. The annual Coal Carrying Championships at Gawthorpe developed from a dispute in 1963 between two patrons of the Beehive public house. The event takes place on Easter Monday and involves men having to carry 55 kg (121 pounds) of coal, and women carrying 20 kg (44 pounds), over a route of almost a mile up a slight hill.

The feast of St Oswald, 5th August, is the date for the annual Church Clipping at **Guiseley**, where he is the patron saint of the parish.

The Sunday school anniversary at **Haworth** on 29th June is marked by a rushbearing ceremony.

A feast on the last Monday of June at **Hepworth** began in 1665 as a thanksgiving for the ending of the plague in the village and as a commemoration of its victims.

Schoolboys at Calder High School, **Midgley**, perform a traditional Pace Egg play on Good Friday, using a text that dates back to the eighteenth century. This resembles other mumming plays and includes such characters as St George, Toss Pot (representing evil), the Doctor and the King of Egypt. Several performances are given in the area throughout the day.

The **Sowerby Bridge** Rushbearing was revived for the Queen's Silver Jubilee in 1977 and has continued ever since. It takes place on the first weekend of September, and the rushcart is paraded through Sowerby, Ripponden, Triangle and Cotton Stones.

The Horse Fair at **Wibsey** near Bradford is still continued, though horse-dealing is no longer a major part of the fair's business. It is now largely a funfair.

Index

Page numbers in italic refer to illustrations